born **AFGHAN**

born **AMERICAN**

born **AGAIN**

By Shahe Nahler

© 2016 by Shahe Nahler

All Rights Reserved

Table of Contents

Acknowledgments 6
Preface 7
Introduction 8
Granny Is Love, God Is Love 9
His Death Brings The Gift Of Life 13
Testimony And Prayer 17
Define Behold 19
Behold 20
No Accident 23
Change 25
Rebellious 28
Bollywood 34
Engagement 36
Marriage 39
Married Life 42
Birth 49
My Passion Is Back 52
It's A Girl 56
Prophetic Trip 59
Aalia's First Birthday 60
Plans 63
New Year's Day 1993 65
Go And See An Attorney 67
Sidetracked-Side Note 69
The Big One 71
The Fight Continues 73

Legally Separated	76
Telling The Family	78
New Beginnings – April 7th, 1993	81
The Summer Of Life And Growth	83
Birth - Round Two	86
It's A Boy!	93
Questioning Everything	96
Television	98
My First Trip To Church	102
First Attempt At Sunday School	107
A New Sunday School Class	111
Judgment House	115
No Peace	121
Know Peace	124
Eyes To See And Ears To Hear	128
The Year Of The Sponge	134
Starving Children In Africa	138
Shovels Vs Spoons	142
I Have Decided To Follow Jesus	146
Welcome To Spiritual Warfare	149
School	151
Burger King Vs The King Of Kings	153
The Mosque	156
I Begin To Work At The Church	160
Court	164
Court - Round Two	169
Single Parent Conference	176

Dancing With My Father And For My Father 183
Adam Makes A Choice 191
An Invitation 197
Books 201

Acknowledgments

How does someone come up with whom to acknowledge in a lifetime? I sit here wondering who I should thank; my husband, my children, and my family? Maybe this person for this, or that person for that, but I keep coming back to just One. The One. The One and Only.

Thank you, God the Father, God the Son (Jesus Christ), and God the Holy Spirit. I realize that I could have just said "God," but I wanted to make sure you knew exactly which "god" I wished to thank.

You have created me. You have lived for me and died for me. You rose again on the third day to prove who You are and what You have conquered. You have redeemed me and saved me from me, and You have made a way for me to spend eternity with You.

To You alone, I am eternally grateful to the Great I Am.

-Shahe Nahler

"Give thanks to the LORD, for He is good; His love endures forever."

Psalm 107:1 (NIV)

Preface

I was born in 1967 in Kabul, Afghanistan.

I have an Afghan father and an American mother.

I have a "citizen born abroad" birth certificate.

I was born with dual citizenship.

I was spiritually born again in 1995.

I have a Heavenly Father and an eternal home.

I have a Savior; His name is Jesus.

This is my testimony of leaving Islam, becoming a Christian, and living a new life in Jesus.

Introduction

I am half way through writing this book, and I have decided to read it to my husband...the second one...the white guy. He is in tears and laughing and states, "You are not right." Then it dawns on me. I am telling you my life, letting you into my not so "right" head and everyone who reads this is going to know-intimately know and understand-my story, my history, and well...me. So you will soon figure out, just like my white husband, that I am not "right." That's kind of scary. To say that I am "normal" is a stretch. To say that I see life through eyes like everyone else is a flat-out lie. I don't. I can't, and I probably never will. I am not the square peg in the round-hole person, but the girl that walks around asking, "Why does my square peg have to go into that round-hole anyway? What if I feel like a triangle today!"

So, bear with me. As I write, I start out timid; scared to let you into my head and heart. As the story goes on, you will discover that what's in my head and heart is "a mess of a girl" who needs to let go of her stuff and let Jesus fill up her heart and head with Him. So, as you read and get to know me, I hope we will become friends, or better yet, become family in Christ Jesus. Then you can tell me your story, too, because we can spend eternity together getting to know-intimately know and understand one another!

Granny Is Love; God Is Love

The earliest memory of God working in my life was while attending Vacation Bible School with my maternal grandmother. I loved my maternal grandmother. She was soft and round with graying curls and a southern accent. She always smelled like Juicy Fruit gum. She was an incredible cook, and her home was always filled with wonderful smells, good food, and family. We lived in the north but we spent summers in the south with Granny. My Granny loved Jesus. My Granny loved her church. So one day, Granny was serving at church so that meant we were too. We got to go to VBS for one day. I remember not even knowing what "VBS" was. I just remember seeing other kids there. We went to the basement of an older red brick Southern church with high basement windows with short, mismatched curtains. Wood paneling was in the rooms filled with small tables and chairs. We heard a story about some guy named Jesus. I got to eat a snack and make a craft. Hello…crafts! I so remember that craft! It was a plain piece of cardboard with a simple flower drawn on it with a black marker. The simple flower was the kind with the circle in the middle and five plump petals. We would spread the glue out and place small colored rocks on the glue. I placed my rocks ever so tenderly. I remember **"loving"** this picture. I remember loving my Granny, so in my little girl way, I wanted to love God too.

The next time I remembered going to church, I must have been around seven years old. We were visiting relatives for the summer. We northern kids were doing the southern summer-thing. This included sleepovers at the cousins' houses. For one set of cousins, it meant a Saturday night sleepover with a visit to church on Sunday. Their dad was the pastor. I didn't know what that meant, but I knew that it was his job, and he had to be there. We wore nice clothes and listened to our uncle speak from up front. I sure looked different from everyone in that room. I sure felt different from everyone in that room. I was very aware of just how different I was when I suddenly felt my aunt nudging me saying, "Honey, these are some pennies for you to put in the birthday jar up front. You have a birthday this week." Pennies in hand, I started to make my way up front for what seemed like the longest aisle walk ever. I didn't like that part. I felt small. I felt different. I placed the pennies in the jar and returned to my seat. Later my aunt explained the tradition to me.

After my uncle had finished talking, we got to go downstairs to some small rooms. All the way down the stairs different people would come up and tell me "Happy Birthday!" We had our lesson; we learned about some guy named Jesus. Before we could leave, my aunt and uncle had to talk to every single person that came that day, and it took forever! But even then, people kept coming up and telling me how glad they were that I was there and happy birthday. I remember feeling special. I remember feeling like I would like to **"belong"** to a place like this where people loved on me even if I was a new face and even if I was afraid to go down the aisle to put pennies in a jar.

I liked church, but we did not go to church. My father and mother were part of the local mosque. We met in an old house downtown near the college campus. It was a very old house. It was not well taken care of, and I used to wonder who had lived here. The men prayed in the living room and dining room, the women in another room. The kids, including my brother and me, ran all over the place. We did, however, play a lot in the basement. One day we were moving boxes of Korans out to our parent's cars. I asked my dad what we were doing. He said today we are moving to a new building. So after some items were loaded into multiple cars and trucks, we set off for the new building.

It was in an older neighborhood filled with houses, sidewalks, mature trees, and older people who lived there. They didn't like what was going on that day. We unpacked the vehicles and started to explore this new building. *Looking back I realize that the "new building" that my father referred to was an old church that was no longer being used. Our group had bought the property and converted it into a mosque.*

It was so different. The main room had a high ceiling covered in wood. There was a strong smell of new carpet in the air. There were two or three steps up to a stage which had one room on each side of it. One of the rooms had a back staircase that led downstairs to the basement. If we went down those stairs, ran through the basement past a lot of little rooms and another small stage and went just past the kitchen, we could come up the other set of stairs to the front foyer. We thought that was so cool. If we went through the foyer just past these funny looking closets full of green robes, we would find an even smaller staircase that led to a balcony. I liked it up there. I could see everything in the main room.

There was a lot to explore up there. There were boxes of music books, music stands, and some pictures in books that had a picture of some guy named Jesus. I remember seeing that book and looking through it. I remember seeing a picture of that man on a wooden cross and wondering who hurt Him and why was he bleeding. I put the book down and looked out across the large main room. Looking past the men praying below, up to the stage I could see a shadow on the wall. Something used to be up there. The light coming into the room revealed the faded lines in the paint that illuminated a cross shape. I remember being **"curious"** and wondering why that cross was taken down. Why did they no longer need their church? Why did they sell it to us?

My family was always doing things related to activities at the mosque. My mom was the mosque secretary, and my father was the president of the mosque for a time. We were always at our mosque. One weekend we were having a special event, a fundraiser. The mosque rented a large local church for a banquet that was to raise money for a mosque being built in Ohio. The men set up the tables and chairs; the women were in the kitchen, and the kids were helping to put the place settings on the tables.

After a long day, we changed our clothes, and lots and lots of people gathered to raise money for the mosque. Being around 10-12 years old, I got stuck with babysitting duties. Someone opened up a very large room for the children to play in. This room was wonderful. There were books, blocks, and toys. There was a wooden kitchen, a wooden baby stroller, and even a wooden iron and ironing board. In fact, there was a whole wooden house set up to play with. It was wonderful. I remember thinking that whoever came to this church must love children because they made such a beautiful room for them to play in. We did not have anything like it at the mosque. As the evening progressed, the parents began to pick up their kids. I remember helping to clean up the toys and feeling sad to leave. I liked being in this church, it felt like **"home."** It felt like Granny and God all rolled up in love.

His Death Brings The Gift Of Life

Everyone knows the story of Santa Claus. Even as a child, being raised in Islam, I knew who Santa was. I knew everything. He had a beard, and red clothes, black boots, and reindeer. I knew some of the songs and watched some shows about him on television. Our local television station even tracked him on radar from the North Pole. I also knew that he loved all the little children of the world and brought them a special gift on Christmas Eve. That is "if" they were good children. Naughty children would get lumps of coal. So, every Christmas as far back as I could remember, I would make a list for Santa and wait for him to come and fill our home with gifts. This never happened of course. My maternal grandparents always sent presents up north to us for Christmas, but Santa never came.

One particular year I was determined to be a "good girl." I set my goal a year ago to be on my best behavior, to be so good that this year Santa would find out how good I was and reward me by showing up and giving me a gift. I was so excited. I went to bed, but I did not sleep. I waited. I listened. I would pop out of bed and look out our apartment window. There was snow on the ground and frost on the windows, and as I leaned on the window, my breath would show. I just knew that this was going to be a special gift. The next morning I got up, looked around our living room (even behind the television), but there were no gifts. I kept hoping all morning. I kept looking out on the balcony wondering if I had some part of the story wrong. Maybe it's because we don't have a fireplace I thought. But slowly I came up with the thought that my idea of being good and what Santa thought was good, must be two different things. I remember being so terribly hurt and disappointed. I remember wondering if Santa loved Muslim children too? As a second grader, I remember associating special gifts with being especially good. The sad thing was because I did not get a **"gift"** from Santa, I thought that I was not good.

Third grade was a whole new world for me. New school, new teacher, new friends, and we moved to a new house. What a different world for a kid whose mother is American and father is from Afghanistan. And so it began, all new teasing from a new round of kids. What kind of name is that? Why is your hair so black? Why do you wear funny clothes? Where did you come from? And on and on, it seemed like I spent my third-grade year answering and re-answering those silly questions. But it was a good year. I liked art, and I had a wonderful music teacher.

The school year ended, and summer began. We found out that my friend Michael, who was nine years old, had slipped from an inner tube and drowned in Fish Lake. I got a note from my teacher in the mail. She wanted to let us know how grateful Michael's parents were for the flowers our class sent in his memory. She went on to say thank you to my mother who so sweetly helped contact the other boys and girls. She also enclosed a small prayer card. The card was a soft purple with pink and white flowers on it. There were also some crosses on it. I used to flip it over and read and reread it. The card asked us to remember his soul in our prayers. It talked about eternal rest for Michael, "may a perpetual light shine upon him," and asking Jesus for mercy.

There comes a moment, a time, an event in our lives that we suddenly realize that there is "life" and there is "death." I heard conversations like, "He is with Jesus now." What did that mean? I had so many unanswered questions. One moment he was here and the next moment he was gone; "permanently gone" was all I understood. I remember Michael's very blonde hair which was so opposite my very black hair. Michael's **"death"** was my moment.

I did not understand death, and no one explained it to me as a child. I can remember learning very specific things with regards to the Islamic faith. Reciting the declaration of faith, memorizing chapters, and learning the stories from the Koran. We took Arabic classes and then went to religion classes that taught us about what we believed. One of those classes taught about the "other" Holy Books. The Jews had the Torah, the Christians had the Bible, but only the Koran was the complete and unchanged word of Allah. Bibles were to be "respected" but not read because they were tainted or changed in the multiple translations. I remember being afraid to touch a Bible because I did not want to "learn something wrong." So I didn't. I obeyed what I learned and did not touch or read a Bible.

One day I was going through my mother's bookshelves. My mother loved to read and had a lot of books. That day I saw a very unfamiliar book. It was covered in white leather. It had golden edges on the paper. It had my mother's name and the words "Holy Bible" printed on the front. It crackled when it opened. The pages seemed to have trouble separating, and I wondered when this book had last been opened. Had this book ever been read? It was so unfamiliar to me. The stiff pages had names I recognized like Abraham and Noah. This book also had lots of words and names that I did not recognize like grace, crucifixion, and resurrection.

The first half of the book kind of reminded me of a distorted version of the Koran. The second half might as well have been written in a foreign language because I could not figure out what they were talking about. I asked my mother where did the golden book come from, and she told me that it was her Bible, and it was a gift to her when she younger. The one part that I did focus in on was the word, life. It seemed like that word was all over that book. I remember reading a small portion that talked about **a new life** and it has to do with some guy named Jesus. The Bible said that His life was a gift.

Time passed, and I had a most wonderful fifth-grade teacher. His love for the humanities and fine arts was willingly shared with us. We went on monthly field trips to museums, churches, parks, and anywhere he could show us local architecture, artwork, music, nature, and dance. I learned the differences in columns and what a flying buttress was. I got to visit a basilica and see the stained glass and learned how each one told a story. I heard music that I had never heard before. I stood before artwork and learned about the different artist and how to tell them apart. My teacher's passion became a part of me. Oh, how I would love to visit him today and tell him what I've seen in recent years, the places where I have traveled and the people I have met. His love for the arts has given me a great foundation.

One particular painting sticks out in my memory. It was an El Greco. He painted elongated figures with dark colors and dark stories. I remember looking up at a very large painting and wondering, what that man did to be hanging on that cross with the people gathered around at his feet? He was bloodied and bruised with His eyes turned upward. His face was in pain, and the people below knew it. I remember thinking, "Why don't they get Him down?" I did not know or intimately understand who He was, but I did somehow sense that it was an important person that should not have to suffer what He was suffering. The title of the painting revealed that it was Jesus on the cross. But I thought the life of Jesus was a gift? If life is a gift, then how can a life of **"suffering"** be a gift?

Testimony And Prayer

Nervous and yet oddly confident, I proceeded to the front of the classroom. I started kind of slowly but built up strength as I started talking. My teacher had asked me to share about my faith in Islam with my classmates. I am sure that not one person in that room knew what I was talking about. I told them the declaration of faith, and about washing and prayers. I went on to explain fasting, giving to the poor, and our pilgrimage. I told them about the holidays, and what we eat and do not eat. They seemed interested, at least as interested as you can be in 6th grade. I sat down, and I remember thinking how great I felt at that moment, sharing about my faith to my friends at school, thinking that maybe one of them might get interested enough to find out more about what I believed in. This memory was the first time I shared my **"testimony,"** because that day I testified in public to be of the faith of Islam. For the next few years of school, I lived my testimony. I was the Muslim kid.

Oh geez, here they come. It was John B., and his friend Tim L. They set their lunch trays down on the table across from me. As they sit down, I remember them immediately talking and asking questions. I had just shared my faith again, this time with my classmates from high school. Tim, John, and I have had many conversations and discussions about religions and faith. They always suckered me in by asking questions about Islam and then talking a lot about some guy whose name is Jesus. I remember wanting to pick up my lunch tray and bolt, but I didn't. My word for this memory would be **"prayer,"** because I politely listened and prayed that someday these two guys would have a passion for Islam the way they do about Jesus. They needed to come to my side, in my mind, since I was right and they were wrong.

What I did not know was that John and Tim and some others had made up a list of ten people that they were going to name specifically in prayers so that those people would one day be saved. Nine boys and one girl. The one girl that they prayed for was me. I never knew I was on their list. I never knew they prayed for me. I never knew I needed to be saved. But God did. And I did get saved. My Savior's Name is Jesus. I used to think how wonderful it would be to one day tap on their shoulders in eternity and say "Surprise! Guess who is here too!" But God had other plans. Better plans. I got to meet up with both of them in this lifetime. What a glorious day to see many years of prayers answered in the salvation of the one you have been praying for. I will tell you that story later, I promise. Never underestimate the power of prayer because if you are praying to the One Who is All-Powerful, then seeds will be planted for a future harvest. He promises. Prayer is powerful and prayer changes things, even one's testimony.

Define Behold

To behold means to see or to perceive.

To behold is to fix one's eyes upon, to see with attention, or to observe with care.

To behold is to see or to observe someone or something, especially of remarkable or impressive nature.

Behold means to pay attention because God is up to something good!

Behold

My senior year of high school is very different. My world is drastically changing because my father has a serious back injury. My parents are distracted by their business, and they are having marriage problems. My brother and I are sort of on our own for the first time in our lives. We are both considered to be responsible kids by our parents, and, because they are so distracted, we can "get away with" a whole lot more than we have in the past. One of those freedoms is that I start being allowed to go to sleepovers at houses of friends' who are not Muslims.

One night I was invited by two friends named Sheri and Sherry to come to one of their homes for the night. I get dropped off by one of my parents and we, in turn, get into a car to go somewhere. I am having so much fun that I do not pay attention to where we are going. We park by a brick church and then get into a small bus with a small group of kids. We drive to another church and meet up with some more kids and get on a bigger bus and drive to a school gym. I have no idea what is going on, but we are laughing and talking and just having fun. Inside the gym, there are bleachers set up and a local music band. We eat pizza and drink pop and play games. It is so much fun. I do not even remember how long we play except that at the end a man gets on a microphone and has everyone come and sit down in the bleachers. He says that he hopes we are having a good time. He hopes that we are enjoying time with friends, but that before it is time to leave he wants to give us a "special kind of hope," one that has a "plan and a future."

I have no idea what he is talking about, but Sheri and Sherry are listening, so I do too. He goes on to tell some stories I don't know, but I listen. He talks about people I don't recognize, but I listen. As he talks, I find myself wondering who are these apostles and disciples and why all of a sudden are we hearing about some guy whose name is Jesus. I cannot even explain at what point my mind "checks in and out" of his talking, but I am hearing and asking, thinking and well…my mind is struggling.

Suddenly I become very unaware of everyone around me and very aware of me. What that man is saying is about me. What he is explaining is about me. What he is trying to share with me is especially for me. My heart is racing, and I ask God all kinds of questions. I am somewhat confused by what my faith is crashing into at this moment, yet so aware that I hear "truth!" My mind and my heart are at war within me. What I "know" and what he says I "need to know" are two different things.

As we leave, I am in tears. I am not ready to leave. I need more. I need someone to explain to me what exactly is going on here. I want what he has. I want "that" which he is talking about, but how can I ask for something like "that?" I do not know what "that" is! Tears. Lots and lots of tears. I feel so very empty and yet want to be full, knowing that what he is offering is what I need, except that I am too scared to say something. My heart is broken, and I am crying.

Now stop for a moment. Looking back I was at a youth event that was set up to share the Gospel with teenagers and their friends that they brought to the church. The activities were great, the band rocked. The pizza and food were devoured. The message of Christ was spot on. So spot on that the target of my heart was hit with not just any hit, but a bulls-eye. Pierced through. Broken. Truth. Truth was shared. The sad thing is that it was not enough! We came, they shared, and we went. Where was the same attention to the follow-up that was paid to setting up the event? Why did a crying girl leave the building with no answers? Why were her unprepared teenage friends expected to share the Gospel with their lost Muslim friend? Where were the prepared and anointed adults that I needed? I needed adults to come and to talk with me, and to answer and explain all of the questions that were raging in me?

After the event, we return to the bus. We are sitting there, one friend on each side and a lost soul in the middle. I am so lost that I do not know how to ask for what I need. I am so broken that I do not know that they have what could heal me. All I know is that "I want that. Whatever it is that they have, I want it."

I fall asleep that night asking God for "that."

Looking back, I realized that in a most basic heart way I wanted Jesus even if I was unprepared to say, Jesus. I wanted what I had heard, and I did not know where to go from there. I did not know it or intimately understand it, but the Holy Spirit was at work within me. The Holy Spirit was stirring my heart, pricking my conscience, and beginning to draw me near to Him. The wondrous part is that God knew what I needed and that I needed Him. He was "that" missing part of my life up until this point and this night would become a starting point in my relationship building journey and process with the Lord. I did not know His Name yet, but He knew mine. He was ok with letting me move forward slowly to find Him. We began a journey together "that" night that will last for eternity!

"Behold, I stand at the door, and knock: if any man hears my voice, and opens the door, I will come in to him, and will sup with him, and he with Me."

Revelation 3:20 (KJV)

No Accident

Do you believe in accidents? I don't. Not anymore. I believe that there is carelessness and that there is recklessness. Both carelessness and recklessness cause accidents. Accidents are just a consequence of someone's actions whether they intend to do that action or not. Don't forget: I'm not a lawyer, just a saved sinner who was once very lost.

My accident was no accident. I was meant to be in an accident that day. "What day?" you ask. Well, it was the one, and only day I missed the activity bus home from school. Don't forget; I did not drive. Seeing what a predicament, I was in, my friend Eric offered me a ride. I kept thinking all the way down to his car, "You cannot do this! You should not be getting into a car with a boy! You are going to get into so much trouble!" Eric then offered to drop me off a few blocks from my parent's restaurant so that my parents would not know that I was riding with him.

Great! Problem solved, I get a ride home, and I won't get into trouble. We arrive at his car, and, as I am climbing in I hear a voice say, "No safety belts." What? Again I hear, "No safety belts." Eric, I ask, "Where are the safety belts?" He laughs and answers that his car is so old that safety belts were not required back then. His car is grandfathered in. What? I have no idea why grandfathers do not want safety belts, but the snow is falling, and the storm is coming. I have missed the bus, and the parking lot is almost empty. I get in and dismiss that voice of warning. We drive onward for what should have been a fifteen-minute drive except that we hit a slick spot at a high speed and then a bump in the road at an intersection. I go head first crashing into the windshield. I am thinking, "So much for a ride home, and I won't get into trouble."

Looking back, it took a hard hit upside my thick head to get my attention. A hard hit through the windshield. If the voice of the Lord warns you, well...you need to listen. To this day I have some physical issues from that disobedient moment. Eric and I would eventually heal physically from the accident, but I could have saved myself a lot of pain and trouble if I would have just listened to that warning. I would not have been hurt. If I had listened to that voice and recognized it as the God of the Universe speaking to my heart, I would have been saved from a lot of pain.

"To whom shall I speak and give warning that they may hear? Behold, their ears are closed and they cannot listen. Behold, the word of the LORD has become a reproach to them; they have no delight in it."

Jeremiah 6:10 (NASB)

Change

The end of the school year is approaching quickly. My school friends are all talking about going to college and what plans they are making for their futures. My Muslim friends are all getting engaged and even married. Once again I am clueless. I promise you I am not a totally clueless person, but it sure feels that way. Being raised Muslim in a non-Muslim country makes me different. Add in being raised with one foreign parent and one American parent makes me even more different. Then throw in a lot of quirkiness, and, well, you are looking at my family and me. We are a southern-touch living in the north, with a huge foreign influence, pretending to be as American as our neighbors. Yup. We are just like you! Ha-ha! We do not do anything remotely "normal."

I graduate with honors, but not engaged. I feel like an old maid at seventeen. It wasn't that there weren't any proposals. It was just that, well...they all basically creeped me out. The Imam at the mosque offered my dad my weight in gold and some camels if I would marry his brother. "Yuk!" I thought, "That guy is almost in his forties! That would be like twenty years older than me!" And there were my friend's brothers...eww, no way! Then there were the men from the mosque... umm...no! And, of the other Afghan guys, my favorite proposal was, "I have four sons, pick anyone you want, but not the oldest one. He is not so smart."

And then there is my family. At my cousin's wedding, a far-off cousin came from California and his family "saw me." They asked my dad if he and I could get married. I remember my dad asking me to go and talk with him during the wedding to see if I would be interested in marrying him. I do not recall anything that poor boy said to me that night. I just kept staring at his eyebrows, well, actually, his eyebrow. It was just one, and it was very long. It went from one side of his face to the other, not even a break at the nose. Uni-brow. So that is what a uni-brow looks like. Then I pictured my future children. Me, at the ripe old age of nineteen having just given birth and about to hold my precious baby boy, the nurse brings him to me and ARGH! The baby had his daddy's uni-brow. My final thought was, "You can pluck that thing you know." And I knew. This was not the relationship into which I wanted to be forever entered, plucking my husband's eyebrow. Not plural unless I plucked! We told them "No." I think my dad said, "I was too young," and probably thinking, "way too immature."

Then there are all of my first cousins. My father was the youngest of nine. I was the last girl born. If any male first cousin older than me was not married yet, I was still their backup bride. The problem was, I had enough American in me that I was way too freaked out about the first cousin and having kids' thing. I had read about hillbillies, and I knew a little bit of nothing to be dangerously forming opinions! Can you imagine those eyebrows?

I still feel bad about one young man. He was shy, and I knew he liked me, but I did not like me, so I could not go there yet. I was determined to learn to drive. I had just turned eighteen, and I thought freedom came from knowing how to drive. Being eighteen it was legal to get your license on your own without your parent's permission, so I had started the process. One evening my family had a whole bunch of other families over to the house at the last minute. We needed bread for an Afghan-style meal, and my dad said I could help by driving up to our restaurant to get the bread. I only had a driving permit, but this particular boy could go with me. We spent time alone for the first time on the drive up and back from the restaurant. Before we got out of the car, he handed me a note that declared his love for me and his future intentions of marriage. I quickly read the note and then tucked it in my pocket and went off to help with the party. Afghans throw great parties. Later my dad found the note, and that was it. Except for one brief moment, I never got to speak to him again. My dad threw a fit, went to their house, said no way, and that was that.

It is almost like a Dr. Seuss book, "Too tall, too small, too thin, too fat, too hairy, too scary, too old, too strict, too Afghan, and too related." I can find a fault in every single proposal that comes my way. It frustrates my family, and it baffles me. It baffles me because I remember thinking how could you marry someone and not even know them. What if I ate children for breakfast? Sounds silly I know, but I am silly. The point is that they did not "know" me, and I did not "know" them. How can I think of marriage when I do not even know what I am doing in August!

Looking back, it amazes me how even when I was not aware of my footsteps, my God was guiding and shepherding my future. At a time when I thought I was in control of my future, the God of the Universe, Who was actually in control, was putting up a hedge of thorns for me not to be able to go this way or that so that I would be positioned for a future in Him.

"Therefore, behold, I will hedge up her way with thorns, and I will build a wall against her so that she cannot find her paths."

Hosea 2:6 (NASB)

Rebellious

What a summer it was! May, I graduated from high school. June, it was my eighteenth birthday. July hosted a big Afghan wedding. Everyone was there. Two Afghan families had children attending the state university. They had decided to get married, so their families threw them a grand wedding. Afghans always throw grand weddings. Lots of people were there, mostly Afghans, but in one corner was an odd bunch. They stuck out like sore thumbs. There were both girls and boys in the corner. Together! You see at our weddings we usually have the women on one side and the men on the other side of the room. Depending on how "religious" you are, determines if there is also a partition in the room. Most of the time they did not because we were considered "modern" Afghans, but it also had to do with the room. A rental room did not always fit the Afghan style of divided sides for men and women.

You do not sit together, so those in the corner were definitely not Afghans. During the wedding, I went to the no man's land, or in this case, the no woman's place in the middle of the room. I was getting a pop, and some of that odd bunch came up to talk to me. Wow, did they stick out! Two boys talking to one girl just does not happen. They were not Afghan, and they had no clue of the social rules. They introduced themselves, and one was very flirty with me. They were international students they explained, friends of the bride and groom from college. They came to the wedding but were unsure of what was going on. So I started to explain the social dynamics of the room.

First, the women dress up, and I mean to the nines! You keep track of what you wear to the weddings so as not to wear the same thing twice too soon. Looks are important. You wear lots of jewels, hair, and make-up, but then most will cover all that up with veils. You get all excited to go to the wedding to see other people, but then when you get there, you sit still and quiet, almost frozen. Everyone wants to be seen in their new outfits, and yet they sit. Older ladies never smile, and the younger ones get in trouble when they do.

The men are even funnier. They sit around so formal, talking, pushing prayer beads as they tell their tales. As Muslims, we are not to drink alcohol. At least that is what you tell everyone, but some totally drink, especially the men. The parties always got more fun after the "non-drinkers" were drunk and started dancing. Afghans are great dancers. Oh yeah, we are not supposed to dance either. But the parties always got more fun after the non-drinking dancers were drunk and started dancing to the music of the non-drinking musicians. They got livelier when they were drunk too. Afghans are great musicians.

The kids just run wild. If the men tell them to stop doing what they are doing, they just run to the women's side and vice versa. There is never any discipline, but always a lot of fun. I explained that the women do not dance with men nor the men with women. I also tell them why some are covered in veils and some are not. The ice was broken, and we just laughed.

Their Brazilian accents were so fun to hear, and I forgot that I was front and center, and all eyes were on me, the unengaged girl in the center of the room with the "foreigners." Insert dramatic music here. They told me their names and the flirty one took my hand and kissed it all the while slipping me his name and phone number on a piece of paper. Whoa. Um. Ok, so suddenly I was snapped back to reality. I quickly withdrew my hand and bolted away. Way too fast. Slightly panicked and hoping no one saw that I returned to the women's side. No one talked to me, so I guessed everyone saw that. I sat there frozen for another hour. The silence was killing me. It was not that the room was silent but that no one would speak to me. I decided to get that drink that I never got the first time.

Returning to the table with my head down and my eyes lowered I quickly picked up a drink and started to move away from the table only to hear a man say, "Did you give that boy your phone number?" I spun around to see an Afghan boy who I knew was interested in me. His face showed that he was hurt and mad all at the same time. I told him "no" and returned to my seat. For the next hour, I sat there smiling and playing with the kids. The women ignored me and that comment haunted me. I felt anger rising while thinking, "I am not married to you. You cannot tell me what to do!" This was not a good combination for a young girl. Rebellion has been brewing in me for eighteen years; growing and waiting to explode was more like it.

I was the dutiful daughter, the obedient child, good grades and good looks, gold stars for good behavior. I made good choices and did good things. I had a good family and good friends and a good house. My world was full of good this and good that but this good girl has had enough "good" and was about to be "un-good" and explode in a not so good way. I stood up with strength previously unknown to me. I moved from the women's side of the room to the drink table to set my punch cup down. I took a quick glance to see if I was noticed and then crossed to the men's side and onto the corner. The corner! The crowded corner filled with international students that were so bored because this was NOT their idea of a wedding party. The corner with the Brazilians in it. The corner I was not supposed to be in because it was the corner with the flirty one.

My heart was pounding as I sat down to the amazement of everyone there. The students were glad to have a new person to chat with, and the Afghans were, well, Afghans. That would come later. We talked about college, and they asked where I was going, and I did not know. It is July they said, "How could I not know where I was going?" They explained all kinds of stuff I had not known. I held the eye of the flirty one. He was from Brazil, and he was so handsome. I stayed in the corner for a couple of hours and then returned to the ladies side shortly before my family was to leave. I broke so many rules that night, but it was also such a rush. The world did not come to an end because I crossed the room. Hell did not freeze over nor did God come to claim me right then and there in front of everyone at the drink table. For now, all was well with the world, and I fell asleep having caught the eye of a handsome man from Brazil.

We got up the next morning and did not go to the mosque. My dad said he did not feel well. Partying does that, but that is not what you admit too. We had a Sunday at home. The phone rang, and I answered it. It was the Afghan boy. "Did you give that man your phone number? You better not call him!" And I hung up. Then I picked up the phone, pulled the note from my pocket and called the Brazilian. We talked briefly and made plans. I went out to lie to my parents. I told them that the call was from my girlfriends, and they wanted me to come over. Any other time in my childhood years this would never have worked, but, I am telling you, my parents were distracted. It was a long season of them being in a distracted place for many reasons, but today they did not say anything but be home before dark.

Again my heart was pounding. I drove 30 minutes to the university and met a boy I had only ever spoken with the night before. This was so unlike me. He took me into this large old university style house with a million rooms and roommates. Everyone, girls, and boys, came and introduced themselves, and he introduced me as his new girlfriend. Girlfriend? Wow, that was quick! I returned a call and met a guy, and now I am a girlfriend! So that's how that works! Half scared and half intrigued, we went out for pizza, and they drank beer. I drank pop. I had a great time. I got my first good night kiss and returned home a triumphant, officially rebellious daughter!

The next day I floated on air. I got a kiss from a handsome man, and I could not let a soul know it. You would think that my parents would have noticed, but, I'm telling you, they were oblivious! For the next three weeks, I became braver. I enrolled myself in a community college near my house and paid for it myself with money I got from my graduation. I began to do things I had never done before, such as planning my future and meeting a boy in secret. Each time I lied, I stayed out longer. Each time I met him we got closer. I wanted to be alone with him. By the end of three weeks, he was getting so serious, and I was getting so afraid of my self-control, or possible lack thereof, that I was physically getting ill. Up until then, we had only ever kissed, but he wanted more. I was not exactly sure how much more, but the one line this "triumphant officially rebellious daughter" was not about to cross was sexual intimacy.

The kiss of death in Islam is to lose your virginity before marriage. I was brave and stupid but not that brave or stupid. I had seen other Afghan girls get that label. The label that is unnamed and unseen but very real. Once you have this label, you do not get married and have children with a "proper man," meaning Afghan or Muslim man. Slim chance, but possible, would be if a foreigner would be willing to take on a "labeled girl." But I so badly wanted to be married and have kids that I was not willing to rebel that much and take a chance on that label. The school was to start next week, and I was about to enter college. In my mind, I was trying to prepare for my future, but my heart was trying to run from my present.

I had plunged myself into something that I did not know how to get out of, so I turned to my trusted friend, "the lie." I lied to my Brazilian boyfriend. I told him that my father was sick with heart trouble and that if he found out, it would kill him. The truth is that he was sick with his back, but he would kill me instead. I had never had a boyfriend or relationship and did not know how I got into this one nor how to get out of it. The truth is I was ashamed of myself, and I was not able to live with the guilt I was feeling about lying to my parents about where I had been and what I had been doing. The truth was that I was ashamed of myself for giving up my first kiss and for getting myself into this situation. The truth was I was not at peace with myself and myself knew it. The truth was that I wanted to go to college, to have a future. I even paid for it myself. The truth was that I felt the need to start clean.

I remember crying all the way home and wondering why it could not work out for us. He even said he loved me and was willing to marry me. But a three-week fling was not the future I wanted to build on. It was now August, and I was starting college.

Later on, I would look back and realize that my secret three-week fling in which I lied to my parents, met with a boy, ate pizza, went to movies, learned to samba, hold hands, and kiss, might have been a secret from my parents even until they read this book. Seriously, they so do not know this yet, but to God, the God Who Knows Everything, it was no secret. He knew what I was doing, and He knew I should not have been doing that, so He took away my peace. I began school so very sorry for my three-week rebellion, but I went in peace because I had told God I was sorry.

"If our hearts condemn us, we know that God is greater than our hearts, and He knows everything."

1 John 3:20 (NIV)

Bollywood

Have you ever heard of Bollywood? It is the nickname for the Indian movie industry as a play on Hollywood, but the industry turns out more films than the west. I grew up going down to the university auditorium. Someone organized the movie on Saturday nights, and we all gathered and watched the latest movies on the big screen. It was wonderful. I grew up with a crush on Amitabh Bachchan and a pocket full of quarters for the candy vending machines at intermission. Intermission, the great break in the middle of the epic drama of a Bollywood movie was always timed to a climactic point with the music dramatically cued to stop at the brink. That meant it was time for candy!

So here is the intermission of my story. I don't want you to be reading along thinking that this girl has it all together and therefore she has somehow figured out on her own how to have a relationship with the Most High God that Created the Universe. On the contrary, I need the intermission placed here because of my stories' climax that you are not yet reading.

I am not making decisions in my life based on obedience to God at this point but on a "peace" and "no peace" basis. You see, Truth has yet to be defined to me. I am in between. I am in transition. I am about to start letting go of a lot of the culture, traditions, and faith that I grew up with and starting to enter a place of wondering "away from" that which I knew. I want to be very clear here. I have not <u>turned</u> toward God. I am starting to look away from the old, but the new is not in my sight.

I am fully aware that when I attend the mosque, my heart is no longer there. My prayers are empty. I wonder if the god to whom I have been praying hears me. I feel like he does not answer. I look around and see people going about life, but not with joy. I see that something is missing, but I do not know what "that" is. I have questions that go unanswered. I have heard a voice that I have yet to grasp is God's. I have begun to be accountable for my actions; to grow up, so to speak, in daily life and take responsibility for myself. I have just begun this journey. So this is the epic, dramatic pause. Run get some candy from the vending machine. Keep reading. It gets better. It gets incredibly better because God is up to something good!

"Taste and see that the Lord is good."

Psalm 34:8 (NIV)

Engagement

August has come, and I have started college. I was timid at first but oddly comfortable in this small community college. I cannot believe I got myself enrolled, bought books and picked out classes all by myself. I have even paid for it with my graduation and birthday money. But now comes the fun part, the second semester is on the horizon. How do I pay for that?

So I put on my new independent self, and I go out to find a job. My parents do not object. They are still distracted. I meet some nice new friends, and we go to the campus center after class. My first time in the door and I immediately notice the people in the corner. More international students. Wait, what? "They are everywhere and always in corners!"

Almost right away some of them begin to talk to me. I look foreign, but they are not sure about me. And over time I make excuses to be in the campus center so that my friends and I can be around them. You would think that a person would learn from their mistakes, but obviously, I didn't learn enough to stay out of corners! So as the semester begins, I have a new school, new job, new friends, and new eyes watching me.

He is from Pakistan. He is tall, dark, handsome, and talks with a bit of a British accent. He tells me how he and some of his friends grew up in the United Arab Emirates. Over time I listen to all his stories of travel, family, and the Muslim world that I know about from afar, but have never seen with my own eyes. His tales are familiar and funny, exciting and exotic. We talk every day at this point, and over the next couple of months, an attraction is birthed as well as a relationship.

What do I think a perfect match for me looks like? I want someone to marry who will let me continue and finish college. I want to remain living in the United States. And the big one, I want to be in a marriage as the "one" wife. What? I know what you are thinking, all marriages have one wife. Well, not in Islam. You can have up to four wives and don't even get me started on the details

36

that go along with and further than, that. He agrees to my wishes, and I agree to get married.

He does the middle-eastern thing and asks my father first for my hand in marriage, and an engagement party is planned. It is so exciting to finally figure out my future. I am so proud of myself for going to school, juggling a job, and homework. I do not talk to God about what I am doing. In fact, I am busy, and I have stopped talking to Him at this point. Being around my future husband reopens my desire to be a "good" Muslim. I desire to be a good Muslim wife and mother. With this encouragement I begin to go backward, getting heavily involved in the mosque again. I start attending the parties and functions. It is exciting now because lots of the focus is on me and my future. As sad as this sounds, I like it being "all about me."

The invitations have all been delivered. Engagements are handled very differently than in the American style. Muslims go all out for engagements because it is another reason to gather and celebrate. These celebrations are just a bit smaller than weddings. Just before the engagement party a friend from college that knows both of us asks to speak with me privately. His name is Michael, Mike for short. He is very serious and nervous about what he is going to tell me. *Bless his heart. I look back and feel his intentions and know that God was using him to try and talk to me.* He wants to talk to me about the man I am going to marry. He goes on to tell me about events, places, people and information he feels that I need to know before getting engaged. He carries a heavy burden, and the Lord is leading him to share his knowledge and the truth with me. He has every intention of having me hear the truth before I get engaged. The problem is me. I do not want to hear the truth. I know I hear the truth because it is that same feeling I had at the youth event. My heart knows what he is saying is the truth, but my head does not want to admit it. I thank him, leave him, and go off to cry.

Pulling myself together I proceed to the building in which my future husband works. I ask to talk with him, and we sit down for a long conversation. One by one I tell him what Michael has said to me. One by one he has a reason, an excuse, or another person to blame for each offense. He takes everything I throw at him, catches it gracefully, wraps it up in a pretty bow, and hands it back to me in a most charming manner. I buy it hook, line, and sinker. Isn't it funny how "sinker" sounds like "sink her?" I take his advice and ignore Michael's warning, brush it off, and get engaged anyway. We have a big party in May. I have just finished my first year of college. I turn nineteen in June and begin to plan for a wedding the next April.

Looking back with clear lenses at this moment, I realize what a forever life lesson this was. If the Lord sends you a messenger (in my case Michael) with a message for you to hear, listen! You need to listen to the messenger and not the one about whom the message is sent. I should never have listened to my future husband, or even to myself for that matter. Listen to the Lord!

Besides, you would think that I would have listened to a sent one, especially one with a name like Michael, but, well, just remember, I said I was an honor student, but I did not say that I was smart!

"My sheep listen to My voice; I know them, and they follow Me."

John 10:27 (NIV)

Marriage

April arrives. Since last May's engagement, we have been planning for our April wedding. School is still happening, but not my relationship with God. I have gone back to my old familiar ways. I decide to be a good Muslim. These past months have been party after party, new clothes, and new plans. We pick out a new place to live which for us, will be an apartment. My parents are participating but still very distracted.

If you wonder why I say distracted, it is just that I respect them greatly, and I have prayed significantly about what will and what will not be entered into this book. I have chosen to leave out anything and everything that is not about what God is doing with me as He pursues me and rescues me as I join into a relationship with Him. He is the focus of the book; I am only in it because He created me. The things I have written are the pivotal points that turn me from the direction I was going to the direction I should be going which is straight to Him. So my parents were distracted and in full wedding planning mode.

His parents arrive a week before the wedding. I have never met them before. I have only talked briefly with them on the phone. They arrive, and with them, the traditions begin. The suitcases were full of new clothes, gifts to be exchanged, jewelry to be given, and sweets to be eaten. There are a whole lot of traditions going on, and, for me, each one is just one step of many in the next week of things that "one just does" when one gets married.

The day has arrived. Today I am getting married. Today is the day I will forever be changed. Today is so busy. Everyone rushes here and there with duties, traditions, "don't forget this," "can't wait for that." The wedding hall is thirty minutes away from our house. At one point just before the ceremony, everyone leaves the house and goes off to the wedding hall. I will be the last to arrive by tradition, and my sweet friend is taking me. There is a calm moment before we leave. My friend goes off downstairs for some final touches, and I am finally alone. All alone. I remember staring in the mirror at myself. I am nineteen years old. I am wearing a golden yellow silk salwar kameez which is a traditional outfit. My hair is fixed, and my makeup was done. I stop and stare at myself for a moment, and I am overwhelmed with a feeling of being alone, or so I thought.

At that moment I clearly hear a still, soft but firm voice say, "Don't do it." What? Don't do what? I think someone is in the room. I look around and stick my head out the door. "Who's there? Is anyone out there?" I just know I heard someone, but no one answers. So I go back to the room. I dismiss the voice with "So this is what having cold feet must mean." I continue to brush my hair, and again I hear, "Don't do it." This time, I am unnerved. "Who's there? Who's in this house?" I call for my friend who comes up from downstairs, and she swears no one else is here, but I know I heard a male voice. She tries to calm me, but there is no use. My peace is gone. I am not talking, "Oh, I have got cold feet or nerves," I mean my peace is gone in that I am shaking, I am about to be ill, and I am about to be late to my wedding.

She drives, and I am shaking. We arrive, and I want to bolt. I have this overwhelming urge to kick off my shoes and run down Highway 10 which is nearby. I feel like I need to physically run until I collapse and with each step toward the building, the need to run grows. I feel like throwing up. I am dripping with nervous sweat as I walk down the stairs of the hall to the room where I will change into my final outfit. Through a small window, I catch a glimpse of the reception hall with all of the people already inside. I am thinking "I don't want to do this," and then in an instant thinking, "but everyone in that room expects me to do this."

We negate the power of culture in our lives. We negate the power of traditions in our lives. We negate the power of people and relationships with those people in our lives. The people pleaser in me did not want to disappoint the people in that room even though the voice said, "Don't do it." My peace is gone, and every part of my being wants to run and never stop, but I do it anyway. I go in. I get married to my Pakistani-Muslim husband. And I begin married life.

Later on in this book, I will give you a look back at this glory moment…sorry, I cannot tell you yet. Keep eating that intermission candy!

"For He is our God, and we are the people of His pasture, and the sheep of His hand. O that today you would listen to His voice!"

Psalm 95:7 (NRS)

Married Life

This chapter is hard to even start. How do you share what went on without sharing what went on? I enter into marriage with the idea that I must be the problem because if I can cook, clean, and dress the part of a good Muslim wife, then I will be a good Muslim wife. I keep thinking that if I just stop trying to be me and be what I am supposed to be, then everything will be just fine. Well, the truth is that it is not fine. I try to leave my husband within the first six months of marriage. I return to my parent's home crying and upset. After I am calm, my mom does what she usually does for problems solving. She gets out a piece of paper and makes a pros and cons list. So we debate my marriage by writing the pros and cons on a piece of paper, and I am sent back to my husband. I come up with the idea that if we are going to improve our relationship and be happy, then we need to move. A clean start, switch apartments because we need a new environment.

The Funny thing is that we only stay at the next apartment for nine months before I want to leave again, and another new start is needed. Change, yes change is good. Maybe, this time, something will fit better. I try to change my surroundings and my circumstances without realizing that God is trying to change me from the inside out. College changes, too. I have finished my associate degree and transfer to a four-year university. This next move will bring us to a university apartment. This new apartment is in a new city with new surroundings. A new school and new friends and a new feeling about my world. My small world grows bigger. I have new ideas flying at me and suddenly walking around this campus I want to be anything but a good Muslim wife. I am not sure what I want to be, but I do not want to be me. I am in huge lecture halls with masses of people and it is a wonderful experience for me. Old libraries with the smell of old books, coffee houses, and rock bands, late night restaurants and college hangouts to overflowing. I see a whole new world that I am not a part of.

I walk everywhere. While walking to class, I pass so many different types of people. The med students with the lab coats, the fine art students with the dramatic black ensemble, and the frat boys with the sports jerseys. They are all traveling on paths they somehow know. Why don't I know where I am going? I only ever walk to and from classes. I walk through the tree-covered pathways and see people walking around with purpose. Why don't I know what my purpose is?

I am studying nutrition, but my passion is not there. I do not like the science classes and the math classes, but I thrive in the psychology and sociology classes. One class, in particular, gets me into more trouble than just my grades. Organic chemistry. Insert dramatic music here, again! I take organic chemistry, and it is above my head. It makes me buckle down and study as I have never studied before, and yet I am making average grades. In many ways, this class is going to both breaks me and make me who I will become someday. The breaking part is letting go of the perfectionist in me and realizing that I better learn enough to pass instead of trying to master something I can barely comprehend. I struggle with each equation, each quiz, and each exam.

About mid-term we are going to have a big exam on some equations. We are given a study guide of equations similar to those that are going to be on the exam. One by one I push through trying to figure out how each works, but I hit a major roadblock. There is this one equation that I have no clue how to solve. I know this one is going to be on the exam, so I panic. I try going to see the teacher, but he is not in. I try the teacher's assistant, but he is not in either. It is now the day before the exam, and I leave a phone message on the TA's machine. "Help!" I plead to that machine. I must have sounded pretty desperate because after I return home, he calls me back.

I take the phone call, and we plan where to meet. Sounds simple enough, right? Well, nothing is ever that simple. I have forgotten to mention that during this time my husband's brother is crashing on our couch. He picks up the phone when I do and without knowing the context of why I am meeting a man, he reports what he has heard to my husband. Not realizing my phone call was between three people, I go off up the street a couple of blocks to MacDonald's. My teacher's assistant has agreed to meet with me for a few minutes to help me, but just until the student he is tutoring shows up because that boy is paying him and he comes first. So I am running. No books in hand; just paper, pencil, and a calculator in my pocket. I run into MacDonald's and sit for ten minutes soaking in everything he says. The other student arrives and upon seeing him come in the main door, my TA says that times up. I get up so relieved that I hug him goodbye and thank him for his help. To me, he is a lifesaver. I will pass this exam. To my brother-in-law who followed me, he is an affair I am meeting, caught in the act of adultery, signed, sealed, and delivered with a hug at the end.

I return to my apartment on cloud nine. I am going to get through an exam that I had been convinced I was going to fail. My husband returns from work and quickly removes me from that high place to remind me who I am supposed to be. Here I again choose not to write. God and I have talked a lot about what to include in this story. My marriage was filled with lots of moments "to not write." The majority of them were "not right." I realize that I have brought you, the reader, to a dramatic point, and then I did not give you the details of that dramatic point. The point is not the drama that happened between my husband and myself, but that this was going to become a pivotal point for God to use this situation to reposition me to find Him.

Ultimately I do not want you to be filled with details about my life but about what God has done in my life. I don't want you to remember who I am but Who God is in my life. But I look back now not with eyes that see because I survived something or because I have 20/20 vision. No, I look back now with the eyes of an overcomer. An overcomer in the Bible is someone who is victorious. I am an overcomer NOT because I won the battle, but because Jesus won it for me. I am an overcomer because of Jesus. I am an overcomer <u>by</u> what Jesus did, and I am an overcomer <u>through</u> what Jesus did. My eyes look back and see Jesus in these moments, and the Jesus that I see is what I choose to write down and glorify. The moments I choose to leave out are the very things that Jesus turned around to bring Himself glory. Glory? How can violence bring about glory? Well, read on dear one!

We have a huge fight. I am accused of everything under the sun without having any idea of the brother-in-law's actions or involvement. I feel like something has hit me out of left field. I am so thrown off that I cannot pull myself together for the exam the next day. In fact, the fight is so huge, at my husband's demand to save our marriage, I withdraw from that college. He is attending a private all-male college nearby, and he tells me that I should transfer to the all-female private college next door to his school. That would keep me away from male teaching assistants, corruption, evil, and all the other trouble I am getting into at MacDonald's. At a loss of what to do, I give in. A part of me is so wounded that my ability to fight back is gone. So I switch schools, and I am now attending an all-girls' private college. So where's the glory I talked about earlier? How can his accusations, slander, and making me change schools somehow bring glory to God? Well at this time, I have no clue. But God does.

The new all-girls' college is another in a long list of environment changes that I think will change me for the better. This time, it is different, and I am about to see a difference, not on the outside, but on the inside. This school is full of girls. Girls with plans. Girls with big plans. These girls are different. They are different from any girls that I have ever come in contact with. They are confident. They are fun and full of life. These girls are single and have jobs, they travel and are talented. These girls have their own checking accounts and cars. They can do whatever they want when they want. At least that is what I see. I come into this school beaten down. I did not want to come here, but I did not want to live in my marriage the way it was at that time either. I study in the campus center, and I find myself people watching. These girls have something I want, and I am determined to get it.

So I study like crazy thinking that is what they have that I do not have. I take a huge load; I stay on campus as much as possible. I want to be surrounded by everything that this school has to offer and find myself wishing I could live here. There is something here, and I just have to figure it out. Part of my heavy class load is that the school requires theology and philosophy classes. Suddenly I am studying other faiths more in depth, and I have to read a Bible for homework. At first, it freaks me out. I even question why I have to read something that I have learned from my childhood is corrupt because it has been translated into so many different languages and written by so many different authors. But if you attend this school, these classes are required, so I obediently read the book. I do not understand it one bit. It reads like the hardest book I have ever picked up. And I thought the organic chemistry was hard!

The hardest part is staying awake. This book has the ability to make me fall asleep as if I have taken a sleeping pill. I even read entire chapters and have no clue what I have just read. Plus the language! I am so *"confuseth that I almost slit-tith my wristeth."* Who talks like this? I seek help before school and after school. I must have driven my teacher mad! Then a paper is assigned. We are supposed to write down what we believe and why we believe it. Sounds easy enough. No one else in the room flinches but me. So I ask the teacher what to do. I do not believe in this Bible so do I have to write about it? She pauses as if praying with her eyes open and slowly grins. "No," she says, "Why don't you write what you personally, believe in. Write from your viewpoint, from your faith, from your soul, write down what you believe in and why." Sounds good to me at the time…until I get home!

I stare at a blank paper for hours. I have the weekend and the weekend is disappearing. Sure I am thinking, I will just write about Islam, it's what I believe in and it's got to be easier than that Bible stuff. This should be *simpleth!* But still, no words come. I start out with a topic such as prayer. I tell about the different prayers and times that we do the prayers. How we act before we do them and what we do after we do them. I explain the act of prayer, but I stumble on the why we pray, or more specifically, the "why I pray." I cannot write down a convincing reason why I pray. You see the assignment is to write down what we believe in and why we believe it. I can do the first part easily. The "what we do" is something that I have known for years. We have a certain way we do things and we are only supposed to do it that way. The "what we do" has an informational reason such as prayers are to be given or spoken to the god of Islam.

But the "why I pray" still stumps me. I pray because I am supposed to. I am supposed to pray five times a day. Honestly, I am not praying, even once a day. I am supposed to say these special words at special times for it to be a prayer. But I stumble in that these are repetitive words, not even my words. I am doing them in Arabic, not even my language. The truth is that this most frustrating paper keeps revealing what I am not doing instead of what I say I believe in.

I hate these kinds of things; the ones that slap me upside the head and make me realize that I am actually wrong. Ugh, I hate being wrong. I hate not being able to write a silly paper for a silly class. I am so frustrated with this paper. Then I remember that I did not choose this school, this school was his idea, meaning my husband's, and then I decide that he should have to write the paper! *Actually, it was His idea, meaning Father God's, and that paper would change me.*

I realize that I cannot write this paper about what I believe in because I do not believe in it. Do you suppose that nun knows that? Do you suppose that grinning nun knows I am stuck in my own mud? I think that little old teacher has something and knows someone that I do not have or know! She knows that to be able to write a paper on belief in something; I have to have a belief in something. This paper reveals the truth, and the truth is that I do not believe in what I was raised in.

Looking back, I realize that my organic chemistry class did change me. It did break me in so many ways. I was broken. My intelligence was not going to get me through. I would be broken from my relationship with my husband. I would take a break from the university, withdraw, and be accepted in the private school. But the class also made me. It made me realize that what I do even with the most innocent intent can be perceived as evil. It made me realize that sometimes we give up our desires and goals to keep the peace. It made me change schools to an all-girls college. It made me be in an environment that had Jesus all over it even if I did not know His Name yet, or that He was "that thing they had that I wanted." It made me take a class that made me put on paper what

I believed in only to find out that I did not believe in what I wrote. I was changing even if I did not realize it was happening.

"Don't copy the behavior and customs of this world, but let God transform you into a new person by changing the way you think. Then you will learn to know God's will for you, which is good and pleasing and perfect."

Romans 12:2 (NLT)

"Don't become so well-adjusted to your culture that you fit into it without even thinking. Instead, fix your attention on God. You'll be changed from the inside out. Readily recognize what He wants from you, and quickly respond to it. Unlike the culture around you, always dragging you down to its level of immaturity, God brings the best out of you, develops well-formed maturity in you."

Romans 12:2 (The Message)

Birth

I have been married now for four years. We are moving again. This time, we are moving into my parents' home in the north. This was the home that I moved to in third grade. My parents have been separated for a while now. She has moved south, and he has been here in the north. He has decided to join her and try and make things work so he moves south and we move into the northern house.

I am changing. I have been letting go of so much lately. I have decided that happiness is not attainable. All religions claim it but their followers keep trying to get to it, or so I think at the time. I am now finishing my third semester at the all-girls' college. My lack of confidence grows as does my abdomen. I am pregnant with my first child. Every visit to the doctor is my attempt to have them tell me if it will be a boy or a girl. But this little person inside of me is an ever moving ball of arms and legs, fingers and toes. They are unable to confirm to me one way or another, but I wonder who this little being is going to be.

I have changed more than my environment again. I have gotten very quiet. I am depressed and lonely. I go to school and see one way of life then come home and live out another. This positioning tears me in two. I want what I cannot have, and what I have I do not want. I have tried to talk to God, but I feel lost. I am no longer praying to the god of Islam because it feels empty. So I am not praying at all. I am not reading anything either. I have moved on from the Bible classes. I pick up no books especially ones called "Holy." I am studying nutrition and the clinical classes in the nursing home are making a newly pregnant mommy-self very ill. The food, the kitchen, the smells, all contribute to making morning sickness into daily sickness. I throw up at the sight of a steak being cut with dripping blood on a TV commercial. Times are hard, and my heart is getting harder.

I finish the semester, talk to my advisor, and she suggests taking time off until the baby is born in September. I can rest in the summer and return to school spring semester. It is just one year.

Little will change in one year. So I listen and obey. I take time off and rest. I am a short person, but it sure feels like I am birthing more than one baby in here. This little being kicks and pokes, moves, and flips. He or she is going to be a challenge, I decide. So much life in here. Why don't I feel "life" out here?

We as a couple have gotten to a roommate kind of status. He goes to work; I go to work. We keep busy, and the busy keeps us apart which is good. We cannot argue or fight when we are apart. Our home life keeps us busy with mowing and housework, but all the while I feel like I have "returned" to a place, this house as if starting over. Did I not learn anything in my time away from this home? Why don't I feel any purpose yet in my life? What plan do I have for my life? Other than a list of college courses to take which defines me by semester intervals, I have no clue who I am or where I am going. I feel like this move home is what I have wanted since the day I got married, yet now that I am home, it is not enough. I want my peace! Where and how do I get peace in my life?

This baby is going to change everything. Now I have to figure me out and parent a child. Maybe this is my purpose. I have seen all the other Afghan women do it. They have lots of kids, they work hard, and they cook and clean and take care of their families. Some are religious and pray five times a day, and some pray only when others are around. That is me. I am pretending right now. I am pretending that I am a Muslim and that everything is ok in my world, or so I portray to others. We go to the parties; we hang out with the Afghan family. It is all fine except that I feel fake. We even go on a picnic to a local state park with the Afghan family. My husband and I have been arguing all day. We decide to take a walk down by the water. The others are thinking we are such a cute couple, but we just do not want to be heard arguing. So we go off and walk. Down by the water, we are walking one way and here comes two guys from my past. It is Tim L. and John B. You remember them don't you? They are the Jesus freaks from high school. We stop and talk a while. I am very pregnant, so they immediately notice. I pretend as if everything is alright and we part ways after talking.

I think how cool it is that they have kept up their friendship and that these four years later they still spend time together. I think that at this season in my life I have kept up with no one from high school. In fact, it is sobering to realize that I am very much alone. I also think how much fun it had been to debate religion and what we believed in. I end my thought process with, "It's a good thing they don't debate me now because my passion is gone. I would have lost that debate, and I don't like to lose."

Looking back I can see why God allowed me to be pregnant during this dark season. Something in me needed to be growing, or there would be death. Having this baby took the focus off of me and put it on this baby. I needed to be focused on growth and life.

"This day I call heaven and earth as witnesses against you that I have set before you life and death, blessings and curses. Now choose life, so that you and your children may live and that you may love the LORD your God, listen to His voice, and hold fast to Him. For the LORD is your life, and He will give you many years in the land He swore to give to your fathers, Abraham, Isaac, and Jacob."

Deuteronomy 30:19-20 (NIV)

My Passion Is Back

My passion is back. My passion is back with a vengeance. It is now the end of summer, and I passionately want to get this baby out of me! It is 1991. The Minnesota Twins are playing the Atlanta Braves in the World Series. The normally fun activity of watching the MLB has been lost in the waves of pain. I came into the hospital yesterday at noon. I find out that I have a heart condition that I previously knew nothing about which will affect my giving birth. Now I become too exhausted to continue the non-progressing labor, so they give me medicine to sleep. I am so out of it this morning. I just remember a nurse gently waking me up and saying she was putting something in my I.V. to speed things along. It is Sunday morning, and I glance over at the clock, and it is 6 am, I start to doze off again, what's Pitocin?

Ahh! Pitocin is a vile medicine that causes chaos in an already chaotic situation. I convince myself that a man has invented this drug and never has any intention of using it on himself because it is sheer evil! Of course, I did nothing "normally". Why change now? I did not take the birthing classes. I did not read all the pregnancy books or talk endlessly about details with my talkative girlfriends. I did the Afghan thing. You just have a baby. Only someone forgot to tell me how to do that part.

I am in this now 24 hours, and I am dying. I am *so* ready to call it quits! I have even asked my mom for a gun, I intend to just shoot myself to be out of my misery, but she jokes that she thinks it best not to oblige because I might kill my husband instead. I hate wisdom. I hate pain. I hate everything right now. They finally agree to give me some painkillers. I start with Demerol. It is supposed to help, but I soon find out that, to my doctors' surprise, there is no relief. Evidently, my body does not react to Demerol, so they try morphine. Good old morphine. I am *so* ready for some rest. I have had contractions every other minute since 6:05 am. "I am never going to have another baby," I swear to myself as I literally try to bend the bedposts.

Time passes and nothing. No pain relief. They call in the doctors and discuss their options. Just get it out I keep thinking. I do not even care anymore if it's a boy or a girl. Just get this thing out. I tell them I have to push, and they rush in, and they say no way, you are only at three centimeters dilated. But I promise them; I feel like I have to push, and then the baby jumps right back up, and it stops. The pain is unbelievable. They want to wait until I am four centimeters dilated until they gave me an epidural but decide to go ahead and give it to me now. "Thank you, Jesus," one nurse says, as they announce their decision. Thank anyone you want right now lady just give me drugs!

They set me up on the side of the bed, tell me how serious it is that I not move because he is going to insert a needle into my spine. Part stupid combined with part exhaustion makes me obey. I sit up; two linebackers dressed as female nurses hold me in a head-locked position to keep me from moving. "What the hell?" I keep thinking. You are squishing me, do you not see the excessively large moving ball in my belly that does not want to be positioned like that. In my anger, I must have changed my body chemistry. I want to knock their socks off and get relief from them, and my body kicks into a full body shake. I am shaking violently. Within seconds more football playing nurses tackle me as if I am holding the game-winning the ball and it is the Super Bowl. The doctor is yelling hold her still, and my body is reacting to the concoction of Demerol, Morphine, and an epidural in me. The doctor is not done yet. I am being held in place with the strength of ten men. I recall hearing, "Hold her down or she will be paralyzed," but nothing in me could stop shaking.

He finishes, I lie back in the bed still shaking, and then every monitor in the room goes off. I am in full distress. I remember it all in a slow motion like haze. The monitor next to me is monitoring the baby and me and, as I watch, the numbers rapidly drop. The nurse must have caught my gaze because she came over and turned the monitor so that I could not read the numbers. In one swift motion what seems like twenty people swarm my bed. My long hair is being tied up and put in a hat. My rings and earrings are being removed. Every piece of clothing is removed, and I am surprised looking down between my legs to see a man that I have never seen before. Whoa. "Who is that?" I ask in my drug-stupid state? The nurse replies that he is the surgical resident that has his arm inserted in me with his fingers between my baby's neck and umbilical cord to keep the baby alive until we get to surgery. At this point, emergency surgery. So that's why I am naked, and my belly is yellow and being shaved. It is all so fast, and now a sheet is being thrown up and over this man and me.

We leave the room in a tent and are whisked down to the surgery. His eyes meet mine in a strange gaze. I am terrified, and he knows it. He just smiles, and I think, "If I live through this I am going to die. I have got a total male stranger down there between my legs." We hit the door, and the rolling bed felt it. I do not remember much after that. A mask, someone near my head talking about their golf game, and then I am out.

They shake me awake for a moment, hold up a bundle of crying baby girl, and take her off to the nursery. I am still drug-stupid, so I think she looks like a little brown baby monkey then I fall back to sleep. At one point I wake up, and someone is counting backward some tools on the table. One female voice jokes, "So how many digits do you have?" I am thinking what's a digit? Then a man speaks up, "What do you mean?" Wait! I know that guy. It is the man from between my legs. The nurse replies, "How many digits do you have? Don't you realize that with the speed that the doctor got the baby out that you could have lost those digits in a split second, and where would your surgical career be without those digits?" I fall asleep with the sight of the doctor looking at his hands and wiggling his fingers with the sudden realization that his career and vast training could have just ended, and thanking God that all was well.

Looking back, I was so unaware of how blessed we both were to have lived through this birth. Both of us came very close to death, but by the grace of God, and the good training of our medical staff, death was avoided for both of us. Think a minute. We encounter people every day that "are very close to death" and yet we walk about in this world "untrained" and "unprepared" to share Jesus with them so that before they die they too would have a hope and a future, a Lord and a Savior.

"For You are my hope; O Lord GOD, You are my confidence from my youth. By You I have been sustained from my birth; You are He who took me from my mother's womb; my praise is continually of You. I have become a marvel to many, for You are my strong refuge. My mouth is filled with Your praise and with Your glory all day long."

Psalm 71: 5-8 (NASB)

It's A Girl

Women are liars. All of them. Ok, so not all of them, just mothers. Mothers are liars. If a woman who has given birth says that it was a wonderful thing, it is such a blessing, oh how precious…she is a liar. I am convinced of it. All that mushy, gushy, lovey talk about the birthing process is hogwash. It hurt, they lied, and I want my money back. That is until they put that little pink monkey in my arms. She is so tiny. Six and a half pounds of a brown baby girl with lots of hair and eyes so dark brown they are almost black. Eyes so black that you can barely see where the iris ends, and the pupil begins. She has ten tiny fingers and ten chubby fat toes (family joke – I'll explain later). Beautiful. I keep thinking; she is just beautiful.

I had picked out the name Aalia. My husband had several other names he wanted, but I would not back down on the name Aalia. There was just something about that name.

We are about to go home after several days in the hospital. The emergency C-section has taken a toll on my body, and I am so tired. The nurse says I can leave after the doctor takes my staples out. So for the next two hours, I panic and sweat, dread and die as I picture the office product that would be removing my staples. What happened to stitches? Who knew? I am about to pass out. It is a chore just to function, and everything is hurting. Plus, throw in that my baby is always hungry and is a terrible breastfeeder.

I struggle to get her to latch on, and when she finally does, she takes two sucks and releases. That only causes the floodgates to open up, and I squirt her in twelve directions. No one tells you these things. I think one hole, one direction, one flow. Who knew? I am crying because I am drowning my brown baby girl with white milk that is all over her and she is crying because, well, I guess because I am. We are a mess, but we are in this together. When she finally starts eating, I relax and just stare at her in awe.

One evening it all changes. She is less than a month old and, did I mention, a terrible breastfeeder? She is doing her normal thing at feeding time. She latches on, takes two sucks, lets go, I start drowning her, she cries, I cry, and we start all over again. This time is particularly rough. I have been feeding her long enough that I am getting very tender in places. I am starting to remember how I think all mothers are liars. It reaffirms my opinion because breastfeeding is supposed to be so "enjoyable." Well, it is not and it hurts! So she is finally eating, and my husband asks for a drink of water. "Get it yourself," I mutter. Now stop. As soon as my words come out of my mouth, I wished I could put them back in again. You do not talk back to your husband, and you always do what he says. He is immediately enraged and gets up and starts throwing a fit as well as everything else in the house that he can get his hands on.

I am now crying with a crying baby at my breast as he turns and yells in my face, "I am going to raise my daughter to obey me, not like your father. He did not do a good enough job with you!" He storms off, and I go in the bedroom with Aalia in tow. I stop crying long enough to get her settled in and eating again. Her eyes are closed as she is getting sleepy as I sit there holding her. She is startled, opens her beautiful dark eyes and looks deep into her mother's eyes as if she knows. I begin to cry and hold her tight and I tell the world that I am not going to raise my daughter the way I was raised. I want to raise her with a hope and a future. Aalia's eyes change me in that moment. I now know what my purpose is. She and I are going to leave. She will be raised differently. I want her to have everything that I do not have and more. I fall asleep knowing that nothing is ever going to be the same again.

Looking back, well, every time I think of this moment I just tear up. This was that moment when life for me changed. I was changed. I was holding my daughter and seeing my life as a female. If I had had a son, I might have thought differently at that moment. But I had a daughter. My daughter needed me to step up to the plate, grow up, and be strong for her. The Lord knew that. He knows me and understands me in all of my silly Shahe-ways. But the good news is that He has a plan, one that involves a hope and a future and the Good News!

"For I know the plans I have for you," declares the LORD, "plans to prosper you and not to harm you, plans to give you hope and a future. Then you will call on me and come and pray to me, and I will listen to you. You will seek me and find me when you seek me with all your heart. I will be found by you," declares the LORD, "and will bring you back from captivity. I will gather you from all the nations and places where I have banished you," declares the LORD, "and will bring you back to the place from which I carried you into exile."

Jeremiah 29:11-14 (NIV)

Prophetic Trip

We take a trip to see my southern family. This is going to be a short comment; I do not remember much except that we took a car trip, my husband, me, and the baby. I am ever so the planner, and I am married to an ever so not the planner person. So to say it is stressful and then add a three-month-old to the picture, well, it is best to keep my comments short. We visit family to introduce them to our baby girl. My uncle is holding her. She has been sleeping softly in his arms for a while now, and everyone knows that there's just nothing better or more precious than holding a sleeping baby. He looks up at me and says that he wishes that we lived closer because it would be so much fun to have her around. Without a thought to my words, I blurt out, "I will have my second baby here."

Looking back I just don't know where that statement came from? I was married, living in the north, no intentions of moving south, but I heard myself say it, and, well, sometimes you have to wonder. I released those words into the universe, from my heart, out of my mouth, and now forever released to the future.

"Guard your steps when you go to the house of God. Go near to listen rather than to offer the sacrifice of fools, who do not know that they do wrong. Do not be quick with your mouth, do not be hasty in your heart to utter anything before God. God is in heaven and you are on earth, so let your words be few. A dream comes when there are many cares, and many words mark the speech of a fool. When you make a vow to God, do not delay to fulfill it. He has no pleasure in fools; fulfill your vow. It is better not to make a vow than to make one and not fulfill it. Do not let your mouth lead you into sin. And do not protest to the temple messenger, "My vow was a mistake." Why should God be angry at what you say and destroy the work of your hands? Much dreaming and many words are meaningless. Therefore fear God."

Ecclesiastes 5:1-7 (NIV)

Aalia's First Birthday

For the past year, my world has revolved around Aalia. She is the light in my dark place. I work and take care of the home and my daughter. I have started thinking about how to leave, but I have not taken any physical actions to go through with it. I concentrate on taking care of Aalia and getting myself healthy and back in shape. My self-esteem is at an all-time low. The only thing I have to look forward to is her first birthday party. It is going to be a Sesame Street birthday party, so I start to plan.

My parents and grandmother drive up to be here for her first birthday. We decide to invite the Afghan family over, and soon it becomes some of the other Afghans as well. Pretty soon the party grows into an all-out bash with his college friends and every other person we can invite in the tristate area. The party is getting out of hand, and I do not have enough hands to have a party. I become extremely stressed out with houseguests, a baby, cooking, cleaning, and a party to host. The more I cook, the more get invited, and that means I have more to cook. The guest list grows too fast, and I cannot keep up. The house is filled to overflowing. It is the end of September, but it is beyond hot in the house. The fear of running out of food and drinks is quickly becoming a reality. There is hardly room to sit and this child's birthday party is becoming a mother's nightmare.

I put her in her rocking chair, pull her up to the small plastic table, and put her cookie monster cake in front of her. We all sing happy birthday, and it is finally about Aalia. I am thinking this night is never going to end. Afghan parties rarely do before midnight, but miraculously, everyone starts to head home, and peace is just a few minutes away. My husband comes up with the great idea that we, he and I, and his college friends all need to go out dancing. I make an excuse for staying with the baby but to no avail. "That's what your parents are for," he says. "They can stay with the baby, and we can go out."

So I tuck my baby girl in bed, take care of my houseguests, and head out with my husband. We go to some bar in some hotel, and it is almost one in the morning. We go in, and it is crowded. He and his friends quickly go off to the dance floor to drink and dance. He starts dancing with some girl, and I am left standing there with no clue what to do. I find an empty table and chair and sit down. I am totally alone.

It has been a very long day, and this loud music is not helping. A man comes over and asks if he can get me something to drink and I say sure a sweet tea. He says he does not have sweet tea, but he does have Long Island Ice Tea. I ask him what that is, and he says it tastes like fruit tea. I agree to it because I like fruit tea. I drink two of those in less than twenty minutes. Think a minute. I am 4'11" and at that time about 110 pounds. I have not eaten all day because I have been too busy. I am hot, tired, and for some reason, this fruit tea is comforting. It does not take long for this non-drinking girl to figure out I am in serious trouble.

The room starts to spin, and I cannot stop it. I ask for help from one of his friends to go and get my husband. I beg to go home, and he becomes angry. One of his friends who knows I do not drink sees the glass and smells it. "What did you drink?" Some fruit tea. "Seriously what was it?" I cannot remember. He gets the waiter, asks him, and finds out that I have had two Long Island Ice Teas. My husband said he would not take me home. He wants to keep dancing so his friend says he will take me. I do not care because I am going to be sick and I just want to leave. His friend helps me out of the place, and we get almost to his car when I fall. He is helping me up as my husband arrives and says he will take me.

He yells at me the whole way home for ruining his evening. I am so carsick and ready to be sick as we finally reach home. We fight. I am upset because my baby, my parents, and my grandmother are inside the house. I drag myself off to the bathroom very incoherent and very sick. While I am sick near the toilet, he takes advantage of the situation. I want nothing more than to throw up on him. I am pushing and fighting and trying to get away from him all the while trying to be quiet because I do not want to wake up the whole house. Something about that night changes my relationship with him as a person. My self-esteem is already at its lowest. It disgusts me, and he disgusts me, and I no longer want anything to do with him. I begin to make real plans to leave.

After typing this and reliving it, I stopped typing for weeks which turned into months. I did not want to continue writing because it just hurt to bring back up all the "old" stuff. I put away the writings for so long that I had forgotten what I wrote. This morning, the Lord reminded me just how much He loves me and said it was time to start again. It is His plan for me to write this. I open it up, read what was previously written, and realize that the next section that I was to write on was "Plans." God has a plan; His plan is for me to share how He pursued me, loved me, died for me, and rose again so that I would learn to seek Him, pray to Him, and love Him. God is so good. His plan is good. I just keep forgetting about Him and His good plans.

"For I know the plans I have for you," declares the LORD, "plans to prosper you and not to harm you, plans to give you hope and a future. Then you will call on me and come and pray to me, and I will listen to you. You will seek me and find me when you seek me with all your heart. I will be found by you," declares the LORD, "and will bring you back from captivity. I will gather you from all the nations and places where I have banished you," declares the LORD, "and will bring you back to the place from which I carried you into exile."

Jeremiah 29:11-14 (NIV)

Plans

After her first birthday party, my mind is made up. I am done, and I am done with him. I do not have a clear long-term plan, but the short-term plan is to go to my parents, tell them I want to leave him and ask them if we can live with them. To pull off this plan, I will need a helper. I speak to my brother who agrees to drive Aalia and me down south to visit our parents for the Christmas break. My husband is working and will not be able to come down. Perfect. So off we drive for fifteen plus hours to stay with my parents for a week. It is Christmas break and snowing in the mountains.

Why is, this time, different than all the other times? I just do not know. But this time, when I ask my parents if I can move in with them and leave my husband they say that it is ok. Relief. For one week I feel relief. Everything will be "done." I will return home, get separated, get divorced, move south, and start over as a single mom. To most that would sound scary but to me it sounds like a relief. We drive over to my Granny's for Christmas. She is a Christian, a sweet, faithful, but feisty little woman who loves her Jesus. We celebrate with all of the American family. We have fun, a big meal, and a tree with presents to open. It is wonderful. I want more of "that" whatever it is that is wonderful. We drive back home. I wake up in the middle of the night. The house is so quiet.

Everyone is sleeping, and I get a drink of water and sit at the top of a long flight of stairs and think about my life. Life is wonderful, and sometimes it is just plain hard, but there is always hope in me. I am not sure why, or how, or even if I can explain it, except that "I believe." I am not sure how long I sit here, but it is a long time. I have peace and a bit of a tummy ache. It must have been all of Granny's green beans I ate.

Looking back, I realize that I have a plan and that God has a plan. Peace comes when I give up on my plans and rest in His plans. Over the years I have realized that His plans are always much better plans than I could have ever come up with on my own.

"You have searched me, LORD, and know me. You know when I sit and when I rise; you perceive my thoughts from afar. You discern my going out and my lying down; you are familiar with all my ways. Before a word is on my tongue you, LORD, know it completely. You hem me in behind and before, you lay your hand upon me. Such knowledge is too wonderful for me, too lofty for me to attain. Where can I go from your Spirit? Where can I flee from your presence? If I go up to the heavens, you are there; if I make my bed in the depths, you are there. If I rise on the wings of the dawn, if I settle on the far side of the sea, even there your hand will guide me, your right hand will hold me fast. If I say, "Surely the darkness will hide me and the light become night around me," even the darkness will not be dark to you; the night will shine like the day, for darkness is as light to you. For you created my inmost being; you knit me together in my mother's womb. I praise you because I am fearfully and wonderfully made; your works are wonderful, I know that full well. My frame was not hidden from you when I was made in the secret place. When I was woven together in the depths of the earth, your eyes saw my unformed body. All the days ordained for me were written in your book before one of them came to be. How precious to me are your thoughts, God! How vast is the sum of them! Were I to count them, they would outnumber the grains of sand-when I awake, I am still with you. If only you, God, would slay the wicked! Away from me, you who are bloodthirsty! They speak of you with evil intent; your adversaries misuse your name. Do I not hate those who hate you, LORD, and abhor those who are in rebellion against you? I have nothing but hatred for them; I count them my enemies. Search me, God, and know my heart; test me and know my anxious thoughts. See if there is any offensive way in me, and lead me in the way everlasting."

Psalm 139 (NIV)

New Year's Day 1993

I am determined to get this over with. So I put my daughter down for a nap and ask to speak to my husband. I calmly tell him how I feel and that I wish to get a divorce. He, in a not so calm way, says no. We argue and fight. This goes on for a couple of weeks. I am tired, worn out, and I have no one to talk too. My Muslim friends advise me to stay married and I cannot. My parents are far away, and they cannot help. I have been away from my American school friends for a long time.

Looking back, I remember being very alone, and every time I would get deeply sad I would hear my baby girl cry or giggle, say a word or take a step. She was a gift and a source of light in a dark and lonely place. I kept thinking of my child and how my child's future would be worth the pain of this. And then hope would return, I would find strength for another day.

"All the commandments that I am commanding you today you shall be careful to do, that you may live and multiply, and go in and possess the land which the LORD swore to give to your forefathers. You shall remember all the ways which the LORD your God has led you in the wilderness these forty years, that He might humble you, testing you, to know what was in your heart, whether you would keep His commandments or not. He humbled you and let you be hungry, and fed you with manna which you did not know, nor did your fathers know, that He might make you understand that man does not live by bread alone, but man lives by everything that proceeds out of the mouth of the LORD. Your clothing did not wear out on you, nor did your foot swell these forty years. Thus you are to know in your heart that the LORD your God was disciplining you just as a man disciplines his son. Therefore, you shall keep the commandments of the LORD your God, to walk in His ways and to fear Him. For the LORD your God is bringing you into a good land, a land of brooks of water, of fountains and springs, flowing forth in valleys and hills; a land of wheat and barley, of vines and fig trees and pomegranates, a land of olive oil and honey; a land where you will eat food without scarcity,

in which you will not lack anything; a land whose stones are iron, and out of whose hills you can dig copper. When you have eaten and are satisfied, you shall bless the LORD your God for the good land which He has given you. Beware that you do not forget the LORD your God by not keeping His commandments and His ordinances and His statutes which I am commanding you today; otherwise, when you have eaten and are satisfied, and have built good house and lived in them, and when your herds and your flocks multiply and your silver and gold multiply, and all that you have multiplies, then your heart will become proud and you will forget the LORD your God who brought you out from the land of Egypt, out of the house of slavery. He led you through the great and terrible wilderness, with its fiery serpents and scorpions and thirsty ground where there was no water; He brought water for you out of the rock of flint. In the wilderness He fed you manna which your fathers did not know, that He might humble you and that He might test you, to do good for you in the end. Otherwise, you may say in your heart, "My power and the strength of my hand made me this wealth." But you shall remember the LORD your God, for it is He who is giving you power to make wealth, that He may confirm His covenant which He swore to your fathers, as it is this day. It shall come about if you ever forget the LORD your God and go after other gods and serve them and worship them, I testify against you today that you will surely perish. Like the nations that the LORD makes to perish before you, so you shall perish; because you would not listen to the voice of the LORD your God."

Deuteronomy Chapter 8 (NASB)

Go And See An Attorney

I remember struggling with how to find an attorney? I remember wanting to find a woman attorney. I remember being scared of a male attorney. I remember entering the attorney's office building and being ready to be sick, but I kept thinking, "I can do this, I can do this." The elevator door opened, and I changed my tune. "I cannot do this; I cannot do this," I thought, but I was in motion.

The door opens, the receptionist greets me, and I wait my turn, meet her, shake hands, and listen. All the while thinking it is just "motion." I tell her why I am here, and she listens. She hands me a background check to fill out along with other information. I fill it out, list assets, list debts, and it is humbling to see your life summarized in paperwork. What are your six years of marriage worth? According to my attorney – eight stapled papers, my signature, and a retainer check.

I return to her a couple of weeks later. The background check has been done, and she has words for me. She starts with that I did not fully disclose all of my debts. She goes on to explain in detail what the background check reveals, but at some point, she must have put two and two together seeing that I am in shock. My face is ashen white, and I sit there dumbfounded in silence. Why? Because I had no previous knowledge of what she is revealing and saying that I have forgotten to tell her. It is all news to me! How much are six years of marriage worth? According to my attorney – now, twenty stapled papers, my signature, and another check.

My sweet friend who is also married to a Muslim watched my baby girl while I went to court. When I get home, I am so tired and drained. I sit on the top of the stairs watching her get her coat on to leave when she turns to me and asks me, "Do you have any regrets?" To which I answer, "Just that Aalia will be an only child."

Looking back I see motion. So far all motion. And now a motion has been filed, and I have asked for a legal separation.

Now I thought everything from this point had been moving right along-motion. But what I did not realize was just how fast this "motion" was going to get.

Motion is defined as the action or process of moving or being moved or of changing place or position, movement. It is also a proposal formally made to a deliberative assembly. I have now filed a legal motion and declared to all who care to listen that I am choosing to leave my marriage. I guess I now have to share it with my family and friends too. The position is important too, recognizing the position you are in and being truthful with yourself about where you are. Pay attention to where God places you. For right now, I am at the top of the stairs. When you are positioned here, and motion causes a change of place or position meaning movement, then the only movement you will experience is falling down. I am about to fall, and the fall is just beginning.

"Then I will go back to my lair until they have borne their guilt and seek My face-in their misery they will earnestly seek Me."

Hosea 5:15 (NIV)

Sidetracked-Side Note

With all of the stress, the arguing, the fighting, the daily life that is ever in motion, I am not feeling well. I am so distracted with the ending of my marriage that my lack of good health is dismissed. That is until one day I just feel awful. I make a doctor's appointment to see my regular physician. Upon arriving, I find that she is on maternity leave, and a retired doctor is helping in her place. He looks nice, like a grandpa with a jolly face. I explain how I have had the flu-like illness for a while and cannot shake it. He listens and tests, pokes and measures, and leave the room. I will never forget his return. "Young lady," he bursts through the door, "You do not have the stomach flu...you are pregnant!" I then "burst" too, only into tears that quickly form a puddle of the mush that is me. Crying and stating that "it was not the green beans at Granny's" he then pulls up a rolling stool, puts his hand on my shoulder, and lets me cry out my troubles to him. He gives me all the time I need. He never acts like I am a bother, nor offers up a comment. When I have unloaded everything, he asks if he can pray for me and he ends it "In Jesus' Name."

I'm typing in tears right now, seems 20 years later that prayer still has power, I know now that the Name of Jesus does. My tears taste salty and yet I do not feel like wiping them away. To do that would be to dismiss them. They are tears that are from the healed broken heart of a girl who still remembers that when she was falling and falling, fast there was a kind man who did not have to take the time to pray with me, but he did.

And that prayer! That amazing prayer that prayed for my future and the future of my children. It still amazes me how God used him to bring me hope and help me to see and hear words that God was in control, that everything would be ok, that God cares, and God loves me very much. I needed to hear that. God knew what I was going through. He loves me. I needed to hear that! That is why I do not wipe away salty tears because to dismiss what God was doing at that moment, but that I was too small to grasp, is huge. What I saw was a fall and a steady path into a deep pit was the very opposite to God's vision. He saw something else. He saw me. He saw my daughter. He saw my new baby. He saw our future in Him. Ahhh! How can you not fall in love with a God that is just that good?

"It is clear to us, friends, that God not only loves you very much but also has put His hand on you for something special."

1 Thessalonians 1:4 (The Message)

The Big One

One of the fights was very memorable. The fight was after asking for a divorce. I was feeding my daughter a bottle (Note the change from breastfeeding and pain) and sitting on the bed. We had been arguing, and he was so upset that he came into the bedroom and started looking for the wedding jewelry. He demanded that it be his because his parents gave it to me. He asked where it was, and I proceeded to explain that the jewelry was given as a gift to the woman so that if ever something were to happen to the husband, the wife would be taken care of. He did not like that answer and got distracted by the fire safe. He was convinced it was in there. "Where is the key?" He would demand, but in the fighting, I could not remember so I told him it was not in there. He did not listen, and he tried to get into the safe. In his frustration, he picked up the heavy safe and threw it at my daughter and me. I remember the sheer panic I felt watching (I guess 50 pounds) headed toward my babies and me. The safe came at me so unexpectedly fast, but, as if in slow motion, it hit the bed in front of us just a few inches away. Instead of bouncing toward us as the motion would have suggested, it stopped and bounced back at him. I think I recall it hurting his foot or something because he got so ticked and stomped off forgetting about us and the safe and the jewelry.

Looking back, I have often replayed that scene in my head. The fastness of the throw and the slowness of the bounce and the complete opposite change of direction than what I expected. In the moment I just saw the physical moment but later with my new eyes, I have always wondered if the Lord did not intervene and protect us at that moment in time.

"Whoever dwells in the shelter of the Most High will rest in the shadow of the Almighty. I will say of the LORD, "He is my refuge and my fortress, my God, in whom I trust." Surely he will save you from the fowler's snare and from the deadly pestilence. He will cover you with his feathers, and under his wings you will find refuge; his faithfulness will be your shield and rampart. You will not fear the terror of night, nor the

arrow that flies by day, nor the pestilence that stalks in the darkness, nor the plague that destroys at midday. A thousand may fall at your side, ten thousand at your right hand, but it will not come near you. You will only observe with your eyes and see the punishment of the wicked. If you say, "The LORD is my refuge," and you make the Most High your dwelling, no harm will overtake you, no disaster will come near your tent. For he will command his angels concerning you to guard you in all your ways; they will lift you up in their hands, so that you will not strike your foot against a stone. You will tread upon the lion and the cobra; you will trample the great lion and the serpent. "Because he loves me," says the LORD, "I will rescue him; I will protect him, for he acknowledges my name. He will call upon me, and I will answer him; I will be with him in trouble, I will deliver him and honor him. With long life will I satisfy him and show him my salvation."

Psalm 91 (NIV)

The Fight Continues

The fight continued, I was so scared and so afraid that I called my brother at work. He worked across the river and was about twenty minutes away, and could not come immediately. So I then called one of my friends who was also married to a Pakistani. Her husband came over immediately and rang the doorbell. I opened the door, and both he and my brother came in. I do not know how they both made it over to our house so quickly, but I was so grateful that they were there. My brother took my husband downstairs to talk. My friend's husband came upstairs with me. We sat down near each other, he on the couch and me in the end chairs. I put my face in my hands and cried. He asked what the fight was about, and I told him that I asked for a divorce.

He proceeded to vomit tons of information about all kinds of things that he thought we must have been fighting about ending with "I knew you would find out about 'that' someday." Again, I apologize to the reader that would like to understand the details but again please understand that God and I have spent much time together with regards to what to write and not to write. Glory, focus on His glory! Well, here I was again, in a position of disbelief and revelation. My face once again gave me away. That is when he realized that he had given me a wealth of information and details that I had no clue about up until that conversation. Did I mention that he was not only my friend's husband but also my husband's friend? Well, he knew more than I did. More tears.

He left. My brother and husband both slept downstairs. I remember checking on my daughter. I left the room that she was sleeping in. I was sobbing. I quietly sobbed so as not to wake her or the others. I sobbed so hard that it hurt my insides. I held my abdomen and sobbed, leaned up against a wall as if it could somehow hug me back and just cried out. I cried out my pains, I wanted to "do something" I thought. Maybe I would throw something but I was entirely too neat and to throw something and break it which would mean that I would also have to be the one to clean it up. I was way too practical for that. I cried out my pains, I wanted to "do something" I thought. Maybe I would scream, but to make noise would be to upset my baby girl, and I was way too maternal for that. I cried out my pains, I wanted to "do something" I thought. Maybe I would get drunk, but to get drunk was not an option because I was pregnant, and I was way too maternal for that too. Besides, I was not a drinker except that one time, and it was not good then either. So I just cried myself out, and when I was at a loss, I turned my body from the wall in which I was seeking comfort and turned so that my back was now against the wall. I let myself slide down the wall until I was sitting there in a pile of me at a loss for what to do next and at that lowered position I cried out to God.

I remember saying something like this, "I need to talk to GOD, the God, and the One Who made me God. I need to talk to the God that made me, and that made the trees and made the universe. I need to talk to the God of the Universe. You are the One that I wish to talk with. My name is Shahe, and You may or may not know me, but I am in a lot of trouble right now. I have no idea what to do, and I have no idea what to say, and I have no idea how to get out of the place that I am in. I need you, not any other god, but YOU, the One Who made me. I need Your help, and I need Your help now…please."

Looking back, I just acknowledged that I needed the God of the Universe. I needed Him in my life. I needed help. I said that I did not know what to do next. I remember suddenly having a feeling of peace and feeling sleepy. I got up, went over and turned off the light, and crawled into bed. Peace had returned, and I got the best night of sleep in weeks. The babies slept too. We all had peace. We were going to need it. We were going to need Him because He is the Prince of Peace.

"Do not let your hearts be troubled; believe in God; believe also in Me. "In my Father's house are many dwelling places; if it were not so, I would have told you; for I go to prepare a place for you. If I go and prepare a place for you, I will come again and receive you to Myself, that where I am, there you may be also. And you know the way where I am going." Thomas said to Him, "Lord, we do not know where You are going, how do we know the way?" Jesus said to him, "I am the

way, and the truth, and the life; no one comes to the Father but through Me. If you had known Me, you would have known My Father also; from now on you know Him and have seen Him." Philip said to Him, "Lord, show us the Father, and it is enough for us." Jesus said to him, "Have I been so long with you, and yet you have not come to know Me, Philip? He who has seen Me has seen the Father; how can you say, 'Show us the Father'? Do you not believe that I am in the Father, and the Father is in Me? The words that I say to you I do not speak on My own initiative, but the Father abiding in Me does His works. Believe Me that I am in the Father and the Father is in Me; otherwise believe because of the works themselves." Truly, truly, I say to you, he who believes in Me, the works that I do, he will do also; greater works than these he will do; because I go to the Father. Whatever you ask in My name, so that the Father may be glorified in the Son. If you ask Me anything in My name, I will do it."

John 14:1-14 (NASB)

Legally Separated

When I found out that I was pregnant, I decided to wait to separate. I knew that being pregnant meant another C-section, and I would need health insurance. So I had resigned myself to staying together until after the baby was born. The idea of staying together only lasted three days which were the longest and most stressful three days I have ever experienced up until this point in my life besides the ever so smooth birth of my daughter.

I found myself holding my breath when he walked into the room and not relaxing and breathing until he left. I could not breathe. I had no peace. I laid crying in bed. My husband did not take the news well. He said that there was no way the baby was his and that I must have cheated on him. I assured him that I did not cheat and that the baby was his, but he still accused me and said that the baby must be the chemistry TA's. What? Him again?

During those three days, when I would turn on the radio, I would hear this song with the words "Don't hang onto the stone it will make you drown." In the car, at the store, even in the doctor's office, everywhere I went this song was playing. It was driving me crazy. I finally decided that I needed to go ahead and leave. I could not decide if the stone was my life, my marriage, or my husband, but I felt like if I hung on to it, I would drown. It felt like God was trying to tell me something because I could not escape it. When I surrendered, I had peace.

We both signed papers. He wanted the car, the television, and the wedding jewelry. I wanted out, Aalia, and the baby. Signing papers and legally being separated was one thing. Living in a home together and asking him to leave physically was another. This did not go well, and my father had to drive up from the south to get him to leave the home. It was an exhausting weekend. All war and no peace. When he finally left there was just numbness. We gathered the Afghan family up on Sunday afternoon to tell them what was going on.

Looking back that was one of the hardest times in my life. I was in a battle that I was unprepared to fight. I was at war with my familiar things like a husband, culture, and traditions. I was also at war with myself. I no longer "knew" what to do or how to do it. I just "knew" that the God who created me was there for me and that I could talk to Him. I "knew" that I did not "know" very much about Him but that He knew everything about me. I was about to have to choose sides, and it was very important for me and the future of my little ones that I choose the side that God was on.

"But let all who take refuge in You be glad, let them ever sing for joy; and may You shelter them, that those who love Your name may exult in You. For it is You who blesses the righteous man, O LORD, You surround him with favor as with a shield."

Psalm 5:11-12 (NASB)

Telling The Family

The family is all gathered; my dad has the adults at the dining room table at one of my cousin's home. I am in the other room taking care of my daughter. He is telling them in Persian what is going on. One by one, arguments, questions, reasons to stay, etc., are being thrown around the table about me and my life, and I am not even included in the conversation. Finally, in frustration holding my baby girl I enter the room, everyone looks up at me and stops talking. "Why stop?" I say. "Say it with me here." My cousin who my parents practically raised since I was four proceeds to tell me that I am about to disgrace and shame our family. No one has ever been divorced in our family. I would be bringing great shame to our family.

One by one I hear mouths full of opinions and accusations. Everything from what did I do to him, so I must be cheating on him, shame on me. I would bring shame to my family. I even get accused that this baby is not his baby. Then my beloved cousin says that I need to get an abortion because I cannot raise a baby on my own and be single. I take all of them, each comment, each negative curse, but that last one from a most beloved cousin who is like my older brother hurts. Standing there holding my baby girl and pregnant with another baby and being told that I need an abortion is more than I could handle. I turn and gather her diaper bag, tell my dad I will be out in the car, and tearfully leave my cousin's home. No goodbyes, no love you, no comfort, and no peace. Just a closed door and a northern winter wind that cut me to my core.

Looking back, I do not know if one ever gets over days like that or words like those. It has taken me hours to write this small chapter, but that moment that door has left a mark on me that still hurts. I had never really thought about abortions until that day. I guess I was of the opinion that every woman should have a choice, but I never had a real definitive answer until that issue was forced on me. Abortion. Me. Why? Why did he say that? Why did he think that? Why can't I have this baby? How could I ever look into my daughter's eyes someday and tell her what I had done and that she would have had a sibling? Or that I listened to my family and not to what I thought was right, and had an abortion. I could not comprehend that comment. It broke me. How could I take a life that I had obviously not planned but was willing to have? Until that moment it was someone else's issue, but at that moment I chose life. I was going to have this baby, and I would definitely be alone in doing so.

This child was a gift because my only regret in the divorce had been that my child would be an only child. Someone heard that regret; someone heard that prayer. God knew. He heard that regret that prayer, that heartbeat that was beating inside me that I did not even know was there that day when my friend asked me if I had any regrets and I replied, "That Aalia would be an only child."

What they saw as shame, I saw as a gift. What they called me, I allowed them to. I never fought back. I never defended myself. To this day, I have had to let go of that day. So when it comes time to write it down, it is hard to pick that awful day back up again. That day the door was slammed shut so hard that it would not open again for many years. To this day most of the family I saw on that day I have never seen or spoken to again. It has been over 20 years. Since that day many doors have been opened and closed in my life. The greatest open door was Jesus. One of the Names of God is "The Door."

"Truly, truly, I say to you, he who does not enter by the door into the fold of the sheep, but climbs up some other way, he is a thief and a robber. But he who enters by the door is as shepherd of the sheep. To him the doorkeeper opens, and the sheep hear his voice, and he calls his own sheep by name and leads them out. When he puts forth all his own, he goes ahead of them, and the sheep follow him because they know his voice." "A stranger they simply will not follow, but will flee from him, because they do not know the voice of strangers." This figure of speech Jesus spoke to them, but they did not understand what those things were which He had been saying to them. So Jesus said to them again, "Truly, truly, I say to you, I am the door of the sheep. All who came before Me are

thieves and robbers, but the sheep did not hear them. I am the door; if anyone enters through Me, he will be saved, and will go in and out and find pasture. The thief comes only to steal and kill and destroy; I came that they may have life, and have it abundantly. I am the good shepherd; the good shepherd lays down His life for the sheep. He who is a hired hand, and not a shepherd, who is not the owner of the sheep, sees the wolf coming, and leaves the sheep and flees, and the wolf snatches them and scatters them. He flees because he is a hired hand and is not concerned about the sheep. I am the good shepherd, and I know My own and My own know Me, even as the Father knows Me and I know the Father; and I lay down My life for the sheep. I have other sheep, which are not of this fold; I must bring them also, and they will hear My voice; and they will become one flock with one shepherd. For this reason the Father loves Me, because I lay down My life so that I may take it again. No one has taken it away from Me, but I lay it down on My own initiative. I have authority to lay it down, and I have authority to take it up again. This commandment I received from My Father." A division occurred again among the Jews because of these words. Many of them were saying, "He has a demon and is insane. Why do you listen to Him?" Others were saying, "These are not the sayings of one demon-possessed. A demon cannot open the eyes of the blind, can he?"

John 10:1-21 (NASB)

New Beginnings – April 7th, 1993

You would think that packing and moving from one state to another would be hard. Especially with a one-year-old and being pregnant, throw in that you are getting divorced and did I mention pregnant? Once papers are signed and the court date is done, it all goes surprisingly easy. I just throw things in boxes. Some boxes I mail by UPS to my parents' home. Some boxes I send with my soon-to-be ex-husband. Some boxes stay with my brother. I do not care at this point. I think I am numb. When you leave like I am leaving there are no good-byes, no farewell parties, and no well wishes. It is almost like you no longer exist to the people in your life. The people you love no longer love you back. Conditional love leaves you numb. There is a great silence. Even my toddler daughter is quiet. She plays quietly in whatever room I am in. If I change rooms, she just follows me with her toys and keeps playing. I am leaving this home with a few bags in my mother's car, a pink snow-suited up baby girl and two ultrasounds have said another baby girl is on the way. With a promise from my brother to mail down Aalia's beloved slide, my mother drives us south. We leave out on a Saturday morning.

It does not take long to figure out that I am pregnant. Every bump on the road for over a thousand miles causes me to have to go to the restroom. We are very slowly leaving the north and heading south. In some ways, it is kind of funny, "If life's roads have bumps…pee." I crack myself up sometimes with the dumbness of me. But humor and trying to see life from a different perspective is the only thing keeping me one step from crazy. We finally give up and pull into a small motel in the middle of nowhere in Illinois. We go into the motel, and the desk clerks are Pakistanis. Of course, "Can't leave home without them," I joke. But seriously, three generations of tired women fall asleep fast only to awake very hungry the next morning.

It is Sunday morning, and we are hungry. This was before the standard breakfast at the motel. We load up the car and start looking for somewhere to eat. Everything is closed. We drive down the road to the next exit. More closures. What is the deal?

Why on this particular Sunday morning is every restaurant and business that we come across is closed? We settle for some gas station snacks to tide us over as we continue down the road looking for more options. Later we find out at a no-name little diner that it is a special Sunday, and the businesses are closed because it is Easter.

Wow, Easter. Who knew? In the throwing of things into boxes, the packing of the car, the frequent rest stops, and the long boring ride, the drive is changing. We went from Saturday to Sunday. We went from cold to warm. The farther south we go, the more clothes are coming off of all of us. Aalia is so happy without that pink snowsuit (which would be the last one she would ever wear). I am changing too. Married to single and it is Easter. Muslims do not celebrate Easter. No bunnies, no colored eggs, no candy. No cross, no empty tomb, and no clue what a resurrection is.

But as we pull into my parent's home, we are greeted by Granny with hugs and kisses. She has new weather appropriate clothes for Aalia, the flowers are blooming, and trees have blossomed so white that as the wind blows, it looks like snow, but the blooms smell like heaven. I leave behind the old me, and the new me is about to be reborn.

Looking back I cannot help but see the joy that the Lord must have had in knowing that I left in death and arrived on His resurrection day. He was about to resurrect me; I just did not know it yet. For right now, I was content with a baby girl playing in the grass, smelling flowers blooming, and seeing life being reborn in the gardens around me.

"Therefore, if anyone is in Christ, he is a new creation; the old has gone, the new has come!"

2 Corinthians 5:17 (NIV)

The Summer Of Life And Growth

We settle into our summer in the south. Sweet tea and my American family. Aalia and I go for walks and play outside. I nap when she naps. My world revolves around her. Every once in a while a phone call from the ex-husband reminds me of what I would like to forget. For a while, just a little while, I would like a break from my life. I do not decorate a baby nursery or have a baby shower like other expectant mothers. No one is excited about my little one coming except me. I struggle to find joy in the little things. Aalia playing with bubbles or an occasional kick from the baby growing inside brings me joy. Flowers and the sunshine, warm breezes and rain bring me comfort. I am not practicing Islam nor am I understanding or walking with the Lord as my Lord and Savior, but I am in this "place" with Him. I just talk to the God of the Universe. I talk to Him a lot. All theology and rules, traditions and regulations set aside. It is me, and it is Him. He is in the flowers; I just know it. He is in the sunshine; I just know it. He is in the wind; I just know it. He is in the rain; I just know it. I find Him in His creations. He is the Creator. I find Him in my toddler daughter and in my little girl to come. I just know it.

"Light is sweet, and it pleases the eyes to see the sun. However many years a man may live, let him enjoy them all. But let him remember the days of darkness, for they will be many. Everything to come is meaningless. Be happy, young man, while you are young, and let your heart give you joy in the days of your youth. Follow the ways of your heart and whatever your eyes see, but know that for all these things God will bring you to judgment. So then, banish anxiety from your heart and cast off the troubles of your body, for youth and vigor are meaningless."

Ecclesiastes 11:7-10 (NIV)

Everything is growing. The trees have switched over from the glorious new green to the deep green that knows how to produce what the tree needs. The flowers have changed from plants to blooms, preparing their seeds for the future harvest. I am growing too. This little one is not so little. Aalia was this ball of energy and movement all curled up in a very little ball. Even very pregnant I did not look very pregnant. But this one is different. Quiet. Calm. I am even shaped differently. I stick out now. From the front, you see a little bump, but my side view is a whole different story. Two more ultrasounds say that this baby is a girl, healthy but quiet. She is growing too.

I find myself seeing God in everything. I have a quiet moment on the front porch, and I can just feel Him. I get anxious and nervous about the future, and something happens to remind me to breathe and be quiet. In a way, my two pregnancies could not be more different. It reminds me of the two lives I have lived. The northern life is a high strung ball of energy, and the southern life is calm and easy going. So I play with my baby girl, wait for my new baby girl, and enjoy the sunshine wondering what changes the end of the summer will bring. I am due on Labor Day.

Summer is here. My friend is getting married at the end of the summer. I search for a meaningful wedding gift to give her, but my money is very limited. I go to the store thinking that I can "make" her something special. I stumble down an aisle with cross stitch. Deciding that this is the route I am going to take, I find a nice poem about love. It reads, "Love is patient, love is kind. It does not envy, it does not boast, it is not proud. It is not rude, it is not self-seeking, it is not easily angered, it keeps no record of wrongs. Love does not delight in evil but rejoices with the truth. It always protects, always trusts, always hopes, always perseveres. Love never fails." It is written by some guy named Corinthians, and he is from St. Paul. Sounds good, sounds impossible, but good enough for a wedding gift. So I buy it and spend the remainder of my time pregnant on bed rest and cross stitching. I never finish it in time for the wedding, so I buy her a crystal bowl instead.

Looking back, I am so glad that I was growing in more than one way. Yes, physically the life in me was becoming a promise yet to be fulfilled. This little one answers the prayer that my daughter would not be an only child. But also the growing from those words that kept me pondering. Patient, kind, trusts? Words that are so definitive like always and never. How about sometimes and maybe? What kind of love am I sewing?

"Love is patient, love is kind. It does not envy, it does not boast, it is not proud. It is not rude, it is not self-seeking, it is not easily angered, it keeps no record of wrongs. Love does not delight in evil but rejoices with the truth. It always protects, always trusts, always hopes, always perseveres. Love never fails."

1 Corinthians 13: 4-8 (NIV)

"And now these three remain: faith, hope, and love. But the greatest of these is love."

1 Corinthians 13:9 (NIV)

Birth - Round Two

Off to the doctor, I go. My visits are weekly, and I still have a couple of weeks to go. My feet are swollen, and the heat is hard to handle in the south. I am very tired, and my doctor announces that my high-risk pregnancy is just that. I need to have this baby soon, so she schedules a C-section for Monday morning. I guess I do not have a couple of weeks left. So I prepare.

I pack my bag and pack my bag for the new baby by filling it up with lots of pink clothes and blankets. Packing such tiny clothes makes me feel somehow in awe of how God creates and grows a little one. I suddenly hear the voices of my Afghan family and being told that I have brought shame on my family and that I cannot be a single mom. In the morning I will become a mother of two. My family did not believe I could be what I am about to be. Then I hear that soft sweet whisper that reminds me that I am already a mother of two and I have been one for a while now. The only difference is what is holding my baby, my arms or my womb. So I settle back into packing pink things. Thank you, God, for the gift of this baby.

The next morning everything is in place. Granny is watching my daughter; my mother takes me to the hospital. It is so different this time. Different seems to be a running theme lately. I have no contractions. I have an appointment. We park our car and walk in calmly. The early morning has several women in the welcome area with panting and paperwork, nervous fathers and frustrations of women in pain. I calmly sign some forms and sit there. Looking around the room at the different faces and wondering what the day ahead will bring. It is just at sunrise and the beams of warm light coming through the big windows. Each of us in that room waits for a nurse to come and get us. Most in that room are praying that they are next as they pant and breath funny.

Then the door opens, a nurse comes back with a chair and heads right for me. I know what the others are thinking. I feel the glares and hear their comments. She's not even in pain. I was here before her. One of my favorites is, "She's smiling, she can't possibly be having a baby!" But the chair is mine. I have an appointment, in by 6 am!

Now the rest of this process is again so very different. I get in and out of beds by myself. I joke when they shave my belly, and I even hop up on the surgical table myself. I am about to be given an epidural, and I am so calm, collected, and composed. The nurses and I are talking; she has seen my paperwork. We discuss so many trivial things like baby names and nail polish. Did I like living in the south? It all seems surreal. I start to think about the last birth situation. The pain, the contractions, the man between my legs, the rush of everything that got me into surgery, and how different this is. I think this is like heaven.

Well, heaven did not last long. In my drifting off into my memories, the anesthesiologist has come in and has begun prepping me for my epidural. I do not think he is ready because he has asked me to lay down on my side. This is nice I think except that I am a little cold. Then everything changes. That sweet soft-spoken nurse and her pro-wrestler nurse friend proceed to follow orders from that sick and wrong doctor and do the smack down on me. In one quick motion, I am tackled, pinned by a pro wrestler into the fetal position and held strong by Samson and her friend Goliath.

Unable to move I holler out, "Hey, there is a baby in there, that does not want to bend!" But it is of no use. In my moment of noise, I feel the epidural, and it HURTS! Unlike any pain, I have ever felt before. What is that? I did not feel THAT last time. Do southern doctors not get the training of the ones in the north? UGH! Why does this hurt so much? "Never again," I swear to myself! No more children! I think about writing a book. The title is, "Liars, it does too hurt," and in it, I plan to demystify and debunk the notion of painless childbirth and the sweet, sick and wrong ladies who smile and coo, and look like they perfectly made it through without messing up their makeup. And it is over. The evil man walks away from me to his equipment. Leaving me in peace and baffled. What was that?

The gang is all here, including my doctor, the nurses, the evil anesthesiologist, and the cardiologist (I have a heart condition). I think, "Let's do this." No contraction is good. No Pitocin is very good. No rushing from one room to the next with a strange man between my legs, priceless. So as surgery begins, I notice smoke. I start to fixate on it. There is a small stream of smoke coming from behind the green tent. The evil anesthesiologist is discussing his golf game with the cardiologist. Do they not see that smoke? I wiggle and get their attention. They move my mask and ask, "If I am feeling anything?" "No, but there is smoke. Something's on fire!" They just grin and say, "It's nothing, don't worry about it." "But I am worried," I reply, "What is on fire?" "Do you really want to know?" the evil one asks. "Yes!" "Well, that is the laser the OB/GYN is using to cut around the scar tissue from your emergency C-section. You have a lot of scar tissue to work around and she is carefully using the laser to cut the layers of flesh to get to the baby." Insert nausea here.

"So when she cuts, the smoke is my flesh?" I tear up. He asks, "Would I like a little more drugs to sleep?" I say, "Yes please." Five seconds pass, and I am in happy land again. I still see the smoke, but, well I don't really care at this point. Then I feel a couple of tugs. They do not hurt because this stuff is good. But I did hear her say, "Oh my, oh my, oh, well look at that!"

What! Look at what! Two heads? Twelve arms? What? What! Look at what! I know that I have been stressed during this pregnancy. I have not exactly been the poster child for keep calm and birth perfect. What? She has everyone's attention in the room, "It's a boy! I have never been wrong before. It's a boy!" Whew. One head. Two arms. A boy. Wait, what? In my drug-induced stupor, I sit there comprehending that the name I had chosen, "Amanda Rose" will be highly inappropriate. I start to fixate again. Who cares about the smoke! It's a boy! Then come the tears, "It's a boy!" I just start to cry. Blame it on the drugs. Blame it on my long nine months of loneliness and rejection. Blame it on the realization of the ramification of having a boy. But the tears are uncontrollable now. It's a boy!

Golf game discussion was in full swing. Yes, I know, I did write that. But the evil one looks down and seeing my flood of tears, moves my oxygen mask and asks me, "Are you ok? Are you feeling anything?" Managing to get out an, "I am fine," I start to blubber. "It's a boy...and I only packed pink dresses for him to wear home from the hospital!" And there it went. Full sobs, the dam, is broken. I let go of the sobs and tears that I have held back for over nine months. That poor evil anesthesiologist. He strokes my hat covered head and tells me it will all be ok. I will be in the hospital for several days, so there is plenty of time to work things out. And he makes this pile of mush of a single mother feel ok again. Yes, I know what you are thinking. He did up the drugs. I fall asleep quickly, and the last thing I can remember is the name, Adam. His name is Adam because he is the first. First what I thought? That's it. I was out.

When I came to in recovery, I remember thinking that I did not get to hold him. So I ask a recovery room nurse who says that if I can move my legs up and down, then I could hold him. So for the next few hours, I try my best to conquer all the drugs that are in me and move my legs. Little did the dumb little me realize that I still have those very drugs in that IV pumping through me, so it is not a win-win situation.

I cleverly figure out a way to move my sheet causing my leg to move so I call her over. She is very impressed. Even stated so. "Now do it without the sheet." Dang it! She's on to me. But I want to see him. Him. It's a boy. It is still such a shocker. Four ultrasounds and four pictures, two different doctors' offices, two different states. How can they all be wrong? But it's a boy! I so want to see him. So as they move me out of recovery to go to my room, they push me past a window with my baby behind the glass. I am so happy to see him. He is pink and huge. That baby is huge. I must still have lots of drugs in me because I keep thinking how grateful I am that this huge baby did not have to come out of me the regular way! Oh, that would have hurt! Can I hold him? Not yet said the nurse. He has to have his bath.

Now you have to realize. I am rather clueless. I went in before 6 am. He was born at 8 am. It is nearly Noon, and I so want to hold this baby boy, but I keep getting, "He has not had his bath yet" comment. How long does it take to bathe a baby? What I do not realize is that they are stalling me. Hours pass. I am doing well. But I have still not seen my baby. I am still hooked up to all kinds of machines that beep. I am getting desperate.

A new nurse, or what I think is a nurse, comes in to fill my water bottle. I ask her if I may please see my baby, and she says she will check. She comes back with a "Honey you cannot see your baby right now because he is in the NICU." And she left. NICU what does that mean? So I am thinking, I know ICU so…and…then overhead speakers, "Code Blue NICU!" "Code Blue NICU." I see people rush past my door, and it hits me, something is wrong; it is my baby boy, and I panic. Now all my heart machines and things start beeping. Now there are people running into my room too.

There are moments in life when you know you are very alone. When you find out things about your husband, and you sink into despair. When your family says that you are a shame to them and you slink away defeated. When the hospital provides a steak dinner for the new parents, and delivers a candlelight meal for two, to a room of a newly divorced mother who will eat alone. I am hungry but choke on each bite because of the tears. When you realize that you are alone, in a hospital room, without your baby in your arms…that is alone. That is when you realize you need God to be with you.

So I plead and beg, beeping all my machines as they work on me. I get calm, and they get to figure out what just happened, so I explain. My nurse, the real one, explains everything. They need me to be calm past a certain point after surgery to protect my heart, so they are stalling in telling me that my baby is in the NICU. He is having trouble breathing and keeping a good temperature. She promises me that he is ok, that the Code Blue is not for him. She tells me that the baby who was Code Blue was also ok. She holds my hand and helps me pull back together and before going promises that she will let me see my baby just as soon as the doctors say it is safe for me to go in there.

She is a kind woman that nurse. She keeps her promise, and by the time I am ready, so is he. She can bring him into my room for a short time. He is huge. He is 7 pounds 6 ounces of a brown baby boy with curly black hair and long eyelashes. He is beautiful. Long fingers, I count every one of them. Long toes (that looked as long as a fingers-family joke), I count every one of them. Such a bundle of blessings! Yes, I count every one of them. We are going to be ok, he and I. We are going to be ok too, HE and I.

Looking back, I cannot help but see the Lord in every step of this birth. Epidurals do hurt, and the first time I had one, I also had other pain killers in my system which helped me not feel the epidural. The Lord helped me by not letting me realize that an epidural does hurt and protecting me from that knowledge because I would be alone and scared. He reminded me that my plans, such as naming a baby Amanda Rose and His plans such as having a son are two different plans. His plans are always better plans! He showed me that protecting the gender of my baby boy was paramount in my ability to leave my situation. The way the Lord hid from earthly eyes the gender of my baby in ultrasound after ultrasound was nothing short of a miracle. No one could orchestrate or plan something so vast without being caught and prosecuted in a court of law. The Lord knew that, and by protecting my son's gender, he protected us both with regards to the courts to come. He reminded me that even when I feel alone, and I am in tears choking on steak, I can cry tears of joy too. Looking back, I think God wanted to emphasize that with me. I could no longer do it all by myself or have the, "I can do it myself attitude." Lesson noted, but it will take a while to say, lesson learned!

"Those who sow in tears will reap with songs of joy."

Psalm 126:5 (NIV)

"For You formed my inward parts; You wove me in my mother's womb. I will give thanks to You, for I am fearfully and wonderfully made; Wonderful are Your works, and my soul knows it very well. My frame was not hidden from You, when I was made in secret, and skillfully wrought in the depths

of the earth; Your eyes have seen my unformed substance; and in Your book were all written the days that were ordained for me, when as yet there was not one of them."

Psalm 139:13-16 (NASB)

"Search me, O God, and know my heart; try me and know my anxious thoughts; and see if there be any hurtful way in me, and lead me in the everlasting way."

Psalm 139:23-23 (NASB)

It's A Boy!

My parents and my Granny have come to visit me in the hospital. They have also brought my sweet baby girl. She is all dressed up in a ruffled dress that grandma has made her. She has a new gift in her arms, a baby doll complete with a bottle and blanket. She shows me her new baby and tells me all about it in her toddler-ease we call "jibber jabber." I show her my new baby too. I show her his little hands and feet and tell her his name is Adam. "Ah dom." She has such a cute way of saying "Ah dom." She wants lots of hugs and kisses, and I struggle with movement. I am worn out just watching her move around the room entertaining everyone with her songs, big smile, and jibber jabber stories about her day. Everyone goes home except Adam and me. It has been a long day. She is simply a bundle of joy. So is Adam. Thank you, God. Thank you, God, for being our Creator. I know You have created me. I know that You have created them. I do not yet know you as well as I should, but I know my name, and I know their names, and somehow deep inside of me, I know that God knows our names too.

"I praise You because I am fearfully and wonderfully made; Your works are wonderful, I know that full well."

Psalm 139:14 (NIV)

The next morning I become a very accomplished woman. I start being able to get out of bed, medical equipment is slowly being removed, and I can eat more than Jell-O. Life is good. I get to hold my baby boy. They ask if I want him circumcised. Well, I never really thought of it before. So they start explaining the procedure and the pros and cons, and somewhere in the blur of the conversation, I just feel a peace about "Yes, he needs to be circumcised." Of course, the ever so clueless me did not realize what that would eventually look like. When it came time to change that first diaper afterward the nurse asked, "Are you going to be ok to do it?" I said, "Yes." That was until I opened the diaper, and it was a NO! I quickly learned to ask for help while there. I could not do it all by myself anymore.

Another funny thing happened. Yes, this time, I knew I had staples. I said I was clueless and oblivious, not stupid. I was prepared for that but was not prepared for my funny nurse. She came in just a roaring with laughter. She was big, and she had big…things. She laughed big and loud and every "things" on her body just wiggled and jiggled when she giggled. She was so full of fun, and I asked her what was so funny. "Girl, I can't go there with you!" More wiggling and jiggling. "No, please" I begged, "What is so funny?" "Girl you would pop your staples if I told you." More begging and more jiggling. "Please!" Finally, she promised to tell me if I promised not to pop my staples. She even put a pillow across my abdomen and made me swear to stay in control. I promise!

So she begins telling me about this frustrated woman who was frustrated with her husband. Ok, I get that, I can relate. She tells me that he had pushed her one too many times, and she lost it. Ok, I can get that too. I can relate. Just one more time. Yup, I've been there done that. She proceeds with the story, "Well, this woman gets a knife and, well (Insert huge jiggling and all-out earthquake of laughter here) and cuts his…off!" What? Ok, I never did that! More laughter, then Lorena (The woman in the story) gets upset and gets in the car and throws *it* out the car window into a field. Then the police come, and they take her husband to the hospital and take her away. Ok, I'm sort of laughing at this point, but my mind is racing trying to understand what the nurse is saying and why it is so funny? It sounds horrific to me. Pain! I'm not good with pain.

Then in tears, she says, "Girl can you see those police officers in that field?" "You pick it up!" "I'm not going to pick it up; you pick it up!" And there it went. Her jiggles, wiggles, and giggles combined with a wonderful accent and storytelling ability, and I lose it. I laugh so hard it hurts, popping staples hurts. She leaves me in tears to continue her rounds. My parents come in for a visit and ask what is so funny. I tell them, obviously without the skill of my beloved nurse, because my Persian father does not laugh. In fact, he sits in the chair and crosses his legs, not even cracking a grin. And yes, if you are wondering, I did pop several staples! I broke my promise to be in control.

The next day while I was packing to leave, I get a special visit from my evil anesthesiologist. He has brought me a present. I am so excited. I tear up the wrapping paper and open the box to find the sweetest baby boy clothes complete with matching shoes. Perfect! Just the perfect outfit to take a baby boy home from the hospital in. He remembered. I felt so bad calling him evil. I did apologize for that. We talked for a while, and he told me that he was praying for my children and me, and for our futures.

Looking back I realize that some problems will come along that are scary, messy, and well more than I can handle, so asking for help is ok. Especially if I ask for His help. Then there are the baby boy clothes. The Lord has often reminded me that what we wear is very important. No, it is not important the color like pink or blue, but the Who we wear that has value. He has value, and He is important to put on daily!

"Rather clothe yourselves in the Lord Jesus Christ."

Romans 13:14 (NIV)

Questioning Everything

For the next season after bringing Adam home, I begin again to question everything. I question simple things like television shows and are they good for my child to watch? To hard things like what should I be teaching my children? I question my past. About my upbringing in Islam, I question my parents, asking them "Why do we believe what we believe?" I ask my parents, my American family, my friends, and neighbors' lots of questions.

I ask everyone but God Himself. Question God? Somehow I had learned that we should never question God. So I did not ask Him. In fact, in my searching over the past eight years since high school, I have changed and questioned virtually every part of my life except God. I have changed schools, jobs, states, marital status, parenting status, addresses, and underwear. I have changed from being a people person who wants to please everyone to no longer trusting anyone. I have changed from clueless to you'd better get a clue! In a way, it seems that I have started on a journey. Right now, with questions, but I have in actuality been journeying for a while now. It has been about eight years going on nine. I have been questioning since my senior year of high school, and I still have no answers. Now my questions have changed. Oh, I still ask my multitude of jibber jabber sounding questions, but I begin to ask them specifically to the God of the Universe. I begin to ask the questions to the One who has the answers.

Looking back I wonder why I was trying so hard not to be me. I was a girl who had questions. I was a girl who asked lots of questions and was willing to keep asking until I got an answer that satisfied me. So why was I not willing to ask God questions? Especially because deep down in me I knew that the God of the Universe had all the answers! I knew that He knew everything! Little did I understand that not only did He have all the answers to my multitudes of questions, but that His answers and His truth would be satisfying to me.

"But if from there you seek the Lord your God, you will find Him if you look for Him with all your heart and with all your soul."

Deuteronomy 4:29 (NIV)

Television

When I first brought Adam home, I attempted to breastfeed for a couple of weeks. I think I made it somewhere between four and six weeks. It was about that time frame when one night I simply did not have any milk left to give him. He was a big boy who really liked to eat. I called the pediatrician who said I could supplement the next feeding by giving him a bottle, but that I should return to breastfeeding the very next feeding time. Ok. I rush to a store and buy formula. Rush home and fix his very first bottle. This poor baby boy is so incredibly hungry that he immediately sucks down six ounces. He just lays there, this brown baby boy with white milk caught in the corner of his mouth. His first baby grin. For the first time in his little baby boy life, he is satisfied to the point of bliss. Yes. He is very milk drunk.

He sleeps for hours and wakes up hungry again. So I nestle him in to feed him. I lift up my shirt, he takes one look at my breasts and starts to cry. He wants nothing to do with me. So now I start to cry. I then give him a bottle which he sucks down with the speed of a NASCAR racecar driver, and I am in pain because I am so ready to feed a baby. In fact, so ready and able that I remember all of the lying mothers again. It hurts, they lied, and I want my money back. AGAIN! Amazing, he weaned in one bottle.

So feeding time with my baby boy becomes something of a challenge. I must make sure he has enough food, work around his newly discovered cow milk allergy, and make sure he does not choke due to the rapidness in which he inhales his food. I am always up for a challenge!

Well, now it is Saturday night. The kids are fed, bathed, cuddled, read to, and tucked into bed and the phone rings. It is my ex. He sounds different. He keeps going on and on about why we are not together and asking why we got a divorce? Ok, so I'm stopping here. What do I say? What to write and to not write? There is so much that I am purposely choosing to leave out that pertains to our marriage because it is ugly. In no way does it bring God glory with the exception that God and God alone brought my children and me out of it, so He alone gets the glory! CS Lewis writes in his book, The Boy and His Horse, that one boy asks why the lion claws the girl. The Voice says, "I am telling you your story, not hers. I tell no one any story but his own," meaning that the Lion has a reason for all he does. So does God. Taking CS Lewis's quote one step further. "It's HIS story."

So I proceed to remind him of the many offenses, and he twists them and says that some of them never even happened. Why would I say those things? So I end up hanging up in frustration. It seems we both have very different sides about what happened in our marriage. In fact, he almost has me believing he is right, and I am wrong, again. "But I did remember," I kept telling myself. My memories of what happened are mine, and I own them, and I know what happened. So I fall asleep questioning again only, this time, a new question. I did not question the memories of events of my marriage like before. I question marriage itself. What is marriage?

The next morning I get up very early to feed my hungry curly headed adorable baby boy with the big brown eyes and even bigger appetite. We, the two of us sit alone in the living room. He eats, and I flip channels on the television. It is very early in the morning in the south. Nothing is on television right now, but church services and preachers. Flip, flip, flip. Stop. This pastor starts off with the question, "What is marriage?" Hold it right there Buster Brown!

I sit up, adjust Adam who is on his way to being happily milk-drunk, and turn the volume up. This pastor is not sweating. He is not yelling. And he does not ask for money. So I decide to listen! He begins telling about Jesus and marriage. How Jesus is our Bridegroom and the church is His Bride. He goes on to tell about how a husband should love his wife like Jesus loves the church. "Well, what does that mean?" I wonder. Then the non-sweating, non-yelling, non-asking for money pastor says, "Let me explain." And he shares and explains Ephesians Chapter 5 verses 15-33. Awe. I am in awe.

Now I realize you think that this not yet saved, rather clueless single mother of two who is a former Muslim, but in the land of "I am a good person," would hear such words of wisdom, understand in full, and all would be well with the world. Well, in my world anyway. But do not forget. I am on a journey, and I have yet to be given "eyes to see and ears to hear." So, I hear "husbands love your wives as Christ loves the church. A husband should love his wife as he loves himself. And a wife should respect and love her husband. That is a good marriage." My question is answered. I asked what marriage is, and I get the answer the very first thing the very next morning. Awesome! And I get the answer, and I do not have to give him any money! Double awesome!

So during the next several weeks, I begin to purpose myself to wake up early enough to feed Adam so that I can watch this guy on television. I do not always understand what he is talking about, but I know I want "that." Again with the "that."

"That" elusive "that" that I cannot verbalize. I do not know how to ask for "that," but I sure want some. So one day while I am watching, the name of the church comes across the bottom of the screen. And since I think all churches are named for the city they are in, I begin to search maps for the name of the church that matches the city it is in. No such luck. Then the next Sunday it has new scrolling words. Ah ha! I know where that is! It is across the street from a very famous hotel in our metro area. I can get there all on my own. After all, I have seen lots of green and white signs that point the way there. So I purposed myself to go there next week!

Looking back, I had a plan. I had found the church. God had a plan too; He is the church!

"Therefore be careful how you walk, not as unwise men but as wise, making the most of your time, because the days are evil. So then do not be foolish, but understand what the will of the Lord is. And do not get drunk with wine, for that is dissipation, but be filled with the Spirit, speaking to one another in psalms and hymns and spiritual songs, singing and making melody with your heart to the Lord; always giving thanks for all things in the name of our Lord Jesus Christ to God, even the Father; and be subject to one another in the fear of Christ. Wives be

subject to your own husbands, as to the Lord. For the husband is the head of the wife, as Christ also is the head of the church, He Himself being the Savior of the body. But as the church is subject to Christ, so also the wives ought to be to their husbands in everything. Husbands, love your wives just as Christ also loved the church and gave Himself up for her, so that He might sanctify her, having cleansed her by the washing of water with the word, that He might present to Himself the church in all her glory, having no spot or wrinkle or any such thing; but that she would be holy and blameless. So husbands ought also to love their own wives as their own bodies. He who loves his own wife loves himself; for no one ever hated his own flesh, but nourishes and cherishes it, just as Christ also does the church, because we are members of His body. For this reason; a man shall leave his father and mother and shall be joined to his wife, and the two shall become one flesh. This mystery is great; but I am speaking with reference to Christ and the church. Nevertheless, each individual among you also is to love his own wife even as himself, and the wife must see to it that she respects her husband."

Ephesians 5:15-33 (NASB)

My First Trip To Church

This is probably one of my most favorite chapters, and I have not even written it yet. But the memories are so warm and funny and the anticipation of trying to put into words the silliness of me is exciting. So here goes. I decide to go to church. I start off like any good churchgoer should by lying to my parents as to where I am going. Yup. I lied. I told my Muslim parents that I was going to go shopping Sunday morning and asked if they would watch the kids for me. Now I come from a long line of cluelessness and obliviousness because in the south, back in 1995, shopping malls and most stores were still closed on Sunday mornings. So shopping should not have been a possibility, but I did not know that and neither did they. I also did not want to take my kids. I did not want to expose them to some kind of cult. I had no idea what I was walking into or where I was going, but I was sure not going to share my beloved children with them. What if they had Kool-Aid! I still remember that kind of church on the news from when I was a kid! I really did think every church or Christian group was a cult.

I also decided to look the part. No foreign clothes! I was going to wear church clothes. I had studied pictures in books and television. I needed a pastel color suit-like ladies dress outfit with a skirt to my knees that was the same color as my jacket and with a flowered blouse underneath. White gloves were nice, but I was not able to find them at the store. I could not find a hat either. I was convinced that I had to have a matching hat. Where do you people buy your hats? Headscarves I can find, hat impossible! But I wanted to blend in and look the part. The funny thing is, I never have, nor ever will blend in! If you know me, then you know exactly how funny that sounds! But I dressed to the best of my ability to look the part. So off I went.

It is the end of summer 1995. I have just spent the summer watching the pastor of this church on television. And here I am ready to go to church. There are lots of cars in the parking lot. This turns out to be a big church. I park the car and start to walk in. I am the only one in the parking lot. I see the main entrance and notice three pretty trees in the front. It seems like an awfully long walkway. I feel like the little child at my uncle's church who didn't want to walk up the aisle with everyone watching me. I can almost feel the birthday pennies in my hand.

As I approach the building, out from behind closed glass doors spring a dozen little old men. White guys are running at me at full speed. It is like a contest to see who can get to me first. Some start to shake my hands. Others are shoving papers in my hands. Others are saying how glad they are that I am here. Still, others are touching my shoulders. All I can do as die inside. You see, in Islam, men do not touch women they do not know and vice versa, and I am surrounded by old white guys, and they are ALL TOUCHING ME! So I am freaking out! I have not said one word. I do reach up and wipe my forehead because I am convinced that it has writing on it saying that "I am a Muslim" or something, and thinking to myself, "Dang it, I wish I had that hat!" I need that hat. I want that hat. Stupid hat!"

I am ushered into the building through wooden double doors into a very large room. They seat me to the back of the room. Last row. This place is packed and just as I sit down so does everyone else in the room. What I do not realize is that the old white guys are ushers. They put me into the sanctuary and since I am late, the service has already started. In fact, unbeknownst to me, the singing, announcements, and introduction to the service were already done. But I was late, and I did not know it. And before I arrived in the sanctuary, the pastor had asked everyone to stand, "To honor the reading of the Word of God," and he read some Bible passage to them. That's when I entered the room and sat down with them.

I have no idea what is going on. Other than my high school graduation, this is the largest number of white people in one room that I have ever sat down with. Ever! I am frozen. My hands are shaking, and I can barely see. I am rather short. Ok, I lied. I am really short. That is no way to start going to church! But I listen as he starts telling a story about a young man who asks his father for his share of the inheritance now instead of when the father dies. This young man then goes out into the world and basically messes up at every turn. In fact, he messes up so much that he ends up in a pig pen. For a former Muslim, this is huge! No one is ever so low as when he is with a pig. Muslims do not do pigs! So I gather that this young man is a real screwed up individual. He sounds a lot like me. Gets out of the house and the first thing he does is mess up his whole life. Man, this sounds like my story. This is so me! But then the pastor stops. He says he will continue the story next week. Wait! Next week? I want to know the end of the story! Wait, I have to come back?

So back I go. Each week for about five or six weeks I go back. I keep going because I want to know what happens! Did the boy go back? Did his father welcome him home? What about the inheritance? Did he get in trouble for wasting it? Did his father forgive him? Why did he throw him a party! I want a party! What about the pigs? I have so many questions!

So I keep going back not knowing that the pastor is reading from a book called the Bible. You see again; I went late every week. Every week, I was attacked physically by old white men. Every week, I tried to find a matching hat to no avail! And every week I lied to my parents about going shopping, but never once did I bring home anything in a shopping bag! You would think that they would ask what I am doing, where do I get money to shop. I have no job! But every week I go back and sit in the same spot just to hear what happens in the story. Boy did that pastor drag out that story! You would think he had made that story into a sermon series or something!

But then it happens. He explains forgiveness, inheritance, welcoming into the family of God, and so much more. The father is ok with the son. I want my father to be ok with his daughter. What I do not realize is that my Heavenly Father is OK with His earthly daughter, I just have not received my inheritance yet!

Looking back, I crack myself up! So silly the things that I thought went along with going to church. Where did I learn such silliness? Probably television! But God knew that I needed every verse of the story of the Prodigal Son explained to me because I had yet to have eyes to see and ears to hear. It was more than a story that I needed to hear, it was my story that I needed to know and intimately understand. I needed to know that the Father welcomed the mess up of a son home again and that all was well again, that he was forgiven and welcomed back into the family. God knew I needed this story explained over time because the relationship He was slowly nurturing in me could not be rushed, but was to be tenderly and lovingly cared for so that it bloom and grow. He is a good God. It is in His very nature to be good and to pursue His children with everything in Him. God will even throw you a party!

"And He said, "A man had two sons. The younger of them said to his father, 'Father, give me the share of the estate that falls to me.' So he divided his wealth between them. And not many days later, the younger son gathered everything together and went on a journey into a distant country, and there he squandered his estate with loose living. Now when he had spent everything, a severe famine occurred in that country, and he began to be impoverished. So he went and hired himself out to one of the citizens of that country, and he sent him into his fields to feed swine. And he would have gladly filled his stomach with the pods that the swine were eating, and no one was giving anything to him. But when he came to his senses, he said, 'How many of my father's hired men have more than enough bread, but I am dying here with hunger!' I will get up and go to my father; and will say to him, "Father, I have sinned against heaven, and in your sight; I am no longer worthy to be called your son; make me as one of your hired men." So he got up and came to his father. But while he was still a long way off, his father saw him and felt compassion for him, and ran and embraced him and kissed him. And the son said to him, 'Father, I have sinned against heaven and in your sight; I am no longer worthy to be called your son.' But the father said to his slaves, 'Quickly bring out the best robe and put it on him, and put a ring on his hand and sandals on his feet; and bring the fattened calf, kill it, and let us eat and celebrate; for this son of mine was dead and has come to life again; he was lost and has been found.' And they began to celebrate. Now his older son was in the field, and when he came and approached the house, he heard music and dancing. And he summoned one of the servants and began inquiring what these things could be. And he said to him, 'Your brother has come, and your father has killed the fattened calf because he has received him back safe and sound.' But he became angry and was not willing to go in; and his father came out and began pleading with him. But he answered and said to his father, 'Look! For so many years I have been serving you and I have never neglected a command of yours; and yet you have never given me a young goat, so that I might celebrate with my friends; but when this son of yours came, who has devoured your wealth with prostitutes, you killed the fattened calf for him.' And he said to him, 'Son, you have always been with me, and all that is mine is yours. But we had to celebrate and rejoice, for this brother of yours was dead and has begun to live, and was lost and has been found.'"

Luke 15:11-32 (NASB)

First Attempt At Sunday School

So now I am a habitual liar. Every Sunday I go shopping when I am actually going to church. I still get attacked by old white guys, but I start to learn some of their names. They do not scare me as much anymore. I still arrive late. I have yet to realize simple things like what a bulletin is and that I should actually read it. That there is an official start time to the service and that the pastor reads from the Bible. I know it sounds funny to you, but it is the truth. I am in a foreign country with no guide. So I watch those people up there on the stage, the ones in the green and white robes. Are they judges? Are they the smart people? Why do they get to sit up there? Why do they leave every time the pastor asks everyone to bow their heads to pray? I think that they think they are clever and sneak out like that hoping no one will notice, but I do. How do I know? Because I never bow my head and close my eyes to pray. I am not there yet. I do not trust these people!

But at the end of this particular service, I hear the pastor say that if anyone wants to meet him after the service, they can come to the welcome center which he explains is just outside the main doors to the right. Great! I can get some of my questions answered! I have so many questions! But upon entering the room, there is a long line formed. I guess other people have lots of questions too. So I stand there not knowing what to do next, and someone guides me to a table. The very unfriendly white-haired lady behind the table huffs and puffs out the question, "Married, single or divorced?" What? Um, divorced. Wham! She writes some number on a piece of paper, and off I go with the guide who pushed me to the table in the first place. He has my elbow and is whisking me through this large brick building filled up with white people. I am totally disoriented as to how I end up in an upstairs room filled with roughly 8-10 women. All but one is crying.

So I sit there frozen. The only non-crying lady in the room comes over and fills out a couple questions on a piece of paper and welcomes me to Sunday school. I am still frozen. But then it happens. "That" shows up. In this small room, the teacher starts to pray. She starts to pour her heart out verbally in a way I have never heard before. Pure, unrehearsed, authentically talking to Jesus and specifically saying His Name. The other ladies have their heads down and eyes closed. Some still tearing up and sniffing, but not me. I want to watch. I do not want to miss "that." I watch her glow. To me, she glows. I surmise that the "that" I am looking for must "glow." That glow is attractive, and it draws me in much like a little bug to the blue light. The bug knows it will die, but willingly releases all control just to bask in "the glow." I feel like a small bug in a large church, trapped in a small room with crying middle-aged women whose husbands have left them for their secretaries.

They are all broken women with broken hearts. The woman that "glows" had been broken too. I can tell by her words that she has been healed. She talks or should I say prays on and on about how the Lord has healed her heart. I keep thinking "It is ok, divorce is ok. I like mine. In time you will stop crying too." What I do have in common with these women is that I have a broken heart too. I have a heart condition that was revealed to me in my early twenties. Physically a heart condition. It is obvious to the teacher and the Lord that I have a spiritual heart condition too. One that only He can heal.

So every week after that I returned to church. Ushered into my seat in the sanctuary. Off to the welcome center. Whisked off at the grumpy lady's command to the small room of divorced women who were twice my age but in a similar position in life. "Sorted by marital status, labeled by an establishment, but not ministered to by name." If it was not for that glowing teacher, I could have missed "that" again.

Week after week she prays her heart out for the ladies. She talks/prays about troubles and putting them in a white box and tying a big red bow on that box and laying it at the feet of Jesus. She describes Jesus. I have never heard anything like "that" before. Words are used like mercy, grace, compassion, beloved, and forgiveness. I cannot define any of them, but I want what she has. I want to have "that" too. I want to be able to picture in my mind to whom I pray. I want to know the one that I pray to, but that- picturing a prophet in your mind (Jesus) is forbidden in Islam. You do not make images or picture Him or any other prophet of God in your mind. I was so instilled in that teaching that it is a struggle each week to let go of the old teachings that I hold on to and go forward to that glowing light.

She really does glow, and the love of the Lord flows out of her and into the room we are in. I cannot tell you a single name of the ladies in that room nor can I picture their faces because the class spends so much time with their heads down in prayer. I can tell you that it birthed in me a desire to glow like my teacher. I never did meet the pastor, not once in all the weeks I went in there to be whisked off upstairs. You see I had to go in the welcome center just to get guided to the room because I never could find that room on my own.

Looking back, I could have easily fallen through the cracks of a large church. Were it not for the authentic romance of my teacher and her Savior that kept me coming back to witness the beauty of His Light in her life, I might not have ever come back. But I did, and God knew who to direct me too. I have spent 12 years on staff at that very church and have blasted many a "process" and "practice" that greets an unbeliever with "Married, single, or divorced." People are not to be sorted or labeled, but known by name and loved on. What if the grumpy white-haired lady in the welcome center was the only person ever to approach me? Then I too would become the grumpy lady who would never come back to this church. I praise the Lord for the Lord's guide who took me to the Lord's anointed one who glowed Jesus, Jesus, and more Jesus. If not for her true love of the Savior who saved her, then I would not have been back to learn more about my Teacher, my Rabbi, my Jesus. My desire to glow like my Teacher Jesus was born in that tiny upper classroom full of tears and broken hearts.

"Who shall separate us from the love of Christ? Shall trouble or hardship or persecution or famine or nakedness or danger or sword? As it is written: "For your sake we face death all day long; we are considered as sheep to be slaughtered." No, in all these things we are more than conquerors through Him who loved us. For I am convinced that neither death nor life, neither angels nor demons, neither the present nor the future,

nor any powers, neither height nor depth, nor anything else in all creation, will be able to separate us from the love of God that is in Christ Jesus our Lord."

Romans 8:35-39 (NIV)

A New Sunday School Class

I faithfully showed up for weeks to my Sunday school class. I began to look forward to hearing from my glowing teacher more than hearing from the pastor because she always went into such detail about Jesus. She would describe Him. Telling me (well others were in the room too) what He was like. She would talk about His characteristics and His life. She would go into such details about this prophet named Jesus. Prophet? Yes, to me He was still a prophet, much like Noah or Abraham, but not the Son of God. But the more time I spent in her room, the more she taught me, the more I started to let go of the words Prophet Jesus, and it became just Jesus. He was all she ever talked about. He was all she ever taught about.

Then one day she comes up to me and says that I am too young to be in her class. That she has been praying about me being in with some younger people more my age. She says she can tell that I am not devastated by my divorce and that I had moved on from it long ago. I kind of giggle. What gave me away? The fact that I am smiling and not crying? That I say divorce is good? I am not sure, but she suggests that I try a class in the chapel, so she walks me down and shows me where to go next week. Ok, do not laugh. I did not know that I could switch classes or rooms if I wished too. I just go where the grumpy white hair lady sent me each week. I wonder if she ever wondered what happened to me when I suddenly stopped showing up at her table? As my friend would say, "Oh well."

Today I sit in the corner of the chapel listening to a new teacher who sits in a circle of people numbering around twelve. I can hardly understand her. She talks with big vocabulary words and uses words that I have no idea what they mean. I am not sure what she is teaching from, and I do not feel welcome. In fact, I feel very alone in a circle of people. But I hear music being played. It comes from behind a rolling partition on the other side of the chapel. I want to be where the laughter and the music is coming from. I do not know why, but I know "that" is over there.

The next Sunday, right after service, I walk myself up to the chapel and sit on the side of the chapel behind the partitions. I am hoping that no one notices that I have moved places. I am hoping that I will feel more welcomed by this group. Hoping that I will once again be on the trail of "that" because "that" is starting to consume me. I still cannot express what "that" is but I sure can tell if someone has "that" or not. I figure out that if I want "that" then I will have to purpose myself to be around the folks that have "that" and hopefully find out what "that" is.

This particular Sunday school class is more my age. It is taught by three young men who are on fire for Jesus. He is all they talk about. They are Kurt, Dewayne, and Cary. Some are in the military and others have enough experience with different faiths and witnessing to recognize that I am not saved. In fact, I must have stuck out big time because they sure seem to be gunning for me every time I show up to class.

Positioning. Being willing to allow God to position you even where you do not know you need to be positioned is very important. Ever since leaving the north, I have let go of trying to "make" things happen. In essence, I have learned to be still. No, not the "and know that He is God" part, but I am getting there, just not yet. I literally do not move until someone actually moves me.

So being moved to this class is important. I move my position on purpose. It feels purposeful. I feel a part of the class from the moment I walk in. It is not that one class is friendlier than the other, although that does have something to do with it. But it is the teaching that positions me and welcomes me. These young guys have the time and energy to invest in the people that attend their class. They allow questions to be asked and boy, do I ask a lot of questions. Especially before and after class and eventually on the phone. I never call to chit chat but to ask a new question.

I will give you an example of what I would ask them. By my house is a church. Sometimes when I drive by there is a white cloth hanging on the cross. Then one day it was black, and now it is purple. Why does the color change? Why does this church always talk about the blood of Jesus? You think Muslims are violent? You people sing about it; you say things like there is power in the blood and victory in the blood of Jesus. You have banners hanging in the sanctuary with blood on them. At least we do not sing about it or decorate the prayer hall with it! And you think we are violent? Why does the lamb have to die? Why a cross? Man, the list goes on. What is the Holy Spirit? Explain that to me, please.

Well, let me just say, you should never teach a class if you are not prepared by God Himself to teach it. Nor should you ever attempt to witness to someone like me if you are not immersed in your Bible! You cannot share what you do not have, and you cannot teach what you do not know! Thankfully, Kurt, Dewayne, and Cary know Jesus, and it shows in how they teach.

Then one day Kurt is teaching, and at the very end, he asks everyone to bow their heads to pray. Well, you know how well I do that. Everyone else obeys and bows their heads and closes their eyes, everyone except me. I want to watch. I am very much still in the observing phase, the non-trusting, you people are so strange in what you do phase, that I never close my eyes!

He then asks the room of thirty-forty people. "If you know without a shadow of a doubt that if you were to die today that you would go to heaven, then raise your hand." Almost everyone raises their hands. Wait, what? How do they know if they get to go to heaven? Did they get a letter? Did angels sing? Violins? Fireworks? How do they know beyond a shadow of a doubt? I want to know that! I want to know if I get to go to heaven too!

Then he says, "Now if you did not raise your hand, do you still have questions or do you not know where you are going if you were to die today? If you would like to talk to someone about those questions, then raise your hand now. No one is looking (well actually I am), so feel free to let us know you have questions, and we will talk to you after class." No one raised their hands. Now, I am pretty sure looking back that they were trying to figure me out. I bet they thought they were clever to do that kind of prayer, but I also bet they had not prepared themselves for the likes of me, because I did not bow my head, nor close my eyes, and I certainly did not raise my hand either time. I am completely baffled by the whole thing. But it does leave me with this desire, "I want to know where I am going after I die?" I want to know if I get to go to heaven!

As class ends, an announcement is made. If anyone wants to go to Judgment House together, we have a reservation and tickets for this coming Saturday night, October 31st, and we can all go together as a class. Class lets out, and I ask what Judgment House is. A girl in the class says it is where you go into the basement of the church, and they turn up the heat, and you feel what hell is like. Um. Ok. I'll go.

So during the next week at home, I am looking forward to my first activity at the church other than on Sunday mornings. This will be my first anything outside of the morning service and Sunday school. But also during the week, I keep talking to God. I talk a lot to God. Not the Holy Spirit, not Jesus the Son of God. I am not there yet. Not even God the Father. I specifically talk to God, the Creator of the Universe Who Created me. I ask the same question all week long. It practically haunts me. I want to know without a shadow of a doubt if I get to go to heaven. God, I want to know if I get to go to heaven.

Looking back it sounds like such a child-like question, "God, I want to know if I get to go to heaven?" But it was what my heart desired. I desired to get to go to heaven when I died.

"Delight yourself in the Lord; and He will give you the desires of your heart."

Psalm 37:4 (NASB)

Judgment House

Saturday comes around very quickly. I arrive at the church to meet up with members of my Sunday school class. This night is very cold, and we are waiting in a tent for what seems like forever. I listen to the people around me, gathering hints of what is to come, but nothing solid. I really have no idea what to expect once we get in there. I do wonder why there are lines of people waiting to get in. Is the basement too small to hold the crowd? Why don't they just do this in the main building which is larger? Anyway, we wait. Soon the line moves, and we are seated in a large room upstairs. Pews have been rearranged to form areas, so groups remain together. I am getting nervous now. I do not know why except that I have observed people coming and getting different groups one at a time and leaving with them. Now it is our turn.

As we go down the stairs, I must seem nervous. Dewayne says that I can stand by him, hold on to him if I need to be reassured. Thanks, but I really have no idea why I need to be reassured. We wind down the stairs and go into a dark basement very slowly and quietly for a large group of people. We enter a small room. Once everyone is in the room, the lights go on, and suddenly there are new people entering the room. They are talking with each other, but not acknowledging us. I have no idea what is going on. Several new people enter into a restaurant situation like a fifty's diner, all talking and carrying on about Jesus and life.

The lights darken and at the same moment a strobe-like light hits, and there is gunfire. At this point, I am unnerved beyond measure. Gunshots! Still not knowing exactly what is happening, part of me wondering when we get to the part where the heat is turned up like hell, and the other part of me is wondering what the hell I am doing here? But the lights come back on, and there are three teens shot and bloodied on the floor, people are crying, and chaos erupts. What is this place? I want out. I now hold on to Dewayne for dear life. Within a few seconds, the lights change again. Everyone I have watched for the past few minute's freezes in place. Wait, what's going on here? The man that led us down the stairs says to follow him.

Winding through a dark hall, we enter another room. What in the world is going on? I am a wreck. But then lights come on, and some of the new people are talking about what just happened. Now I get it. It is some kind of play that is unlike any I have seen before. There are fifteen-twenty of us lined up against a wall watching a few people in a room. The actors are talking about the teens dying. I have no idea what they are saying because I am so unnerved. Dewayne is there beside me, and then the lights turn off, and we move to other rooms.

Room by room we wind through this basement; dark halls, lights on, action, lights off, move rooms. We are like flies on the wall, quietly watching lives lived out in front of us. We do not speak and they, the actors, never acknowledge that we are there. All I can tell is that there are discussions about the dead teens and how each of them dealt with Jesus.

Now we enter a new room. Smaller and draped in black curtains. Somehow, in the shifting from room to room, I have lost Dewayne. I feel very alone. This room is lit only by stinky candles. Lots of smells mix to make one giant yuk of odor. Everyone from our group waits quietly for the lights, but this time, it is different. A wall or curtain moves and a chair with a man in it comes around a turntable kind of thing. He comes out of his chair just as others dressed in black enter from a back door. There is lots of yelling and chaos, and someone pushes a girl in a rolling cage into the room. Now at this point, I recognize the girl in the cage. She is one of the dead teens. She is crying and very upset. Then other actors in black bring in one of the other dead teens and push her to the feet of the man in black, the one that came out of the darkness.

He is yelling at her, and she is begging. Both girls are crying and begging. He laughs and taunts them. He is telling them, "Welcome to hell," and seems to be so proud that they are there. One of the dead teens starts asking why she is there. She went to church, she read her Bible, stating that she comes from a Christian family. Why is she there she begs of him? With a most evil laugh, he turns on her. My heart breaks for this teen. I don't understand it either. She is the "good one," or so I had surmised from the play dialogue. I get the other teen; she rejected Jesus in the diner. She did not want anything to do with Him, so, for some strange reason, I get why she is there. But this one that is crying and begging, I don't understand! I am so upset for her. *God, I am so confused!*

Then the man from the darkness, who I have guessed is the devil, starts yelling how the one teen was easy to "get" because she rejected Jesus, but that the girl at his feet, she is the real catch because he was able to keep her from a making a decision for Jesus. Then he suddenly turns right to me, heads right over to me. So far, not in one single room of many did a single actor acknowledge that we were there, up against the wall like bugs. But now! What the hell? I am panicking! He so gets up right into my face, looks me in my eyes, still yelling at the girl and leans in on me! Me! Leans! I bend backward and away, smelling the yuk of the candles, hearing all the yelling and crying of the girls. There is laughter coming from the actors in black, which I have guessed are his helpers. He leans in on me. "You are going to hell!" Right in my face. No one else. He never acknowledges anyone else. Just me! Ugh! But as he pulls away from me slowly, I have this "thought." "You are going to hell," he says again. To which I reply in my head, "Shhhh, I know, I know, don't tell anyone!" And he turns away. I am so upset because I feel as if everyone in the room knows my inner secret. I have been exposed. I am naked and ashamed and know without a shadow of a doubt that I am going to hell. Lights on, we start to move. Where is Dewayne?

We move into a completely opposite room. It is large and decorated with everything white. No stinky candles, but there are people dressed in white robes, and soft music is playing in the background. My head is still spinning from the devil yelling at me when I come out of my fog to see a little girl twirling in a tutu around the room. A little ballerina. You people have a devil in the basement and a ballerina in a white room. I am done. I want out, but I am ever so far from the door. Trapped! Dang it! Then a curtain moves, and I see the third dead teen come into the room. She is immediately greeted by people she knows. Smiles, kisses, and warm embraces. She joins them and turns to the door again. I turn too. No longer distracted by the ballerina, I turn to the door to see "Him."

He is a man dress in a white robe with a crown and a sash. He is dressed up to look like the Jesus my beloved Sunday school teacher spoke of in that small upper classroom. He is radiant and greets the teenager. Then he turns and heads right for me. What is going on here! He comes directly over to me and takes my hand, pulls it to him and looks me right in the eyes. I feel the makeup on his hands in my hands. The ones that make it seem like he was pierced by large nails, but his hands are warm, and he won't let go. When my eyes finally meet his, I feel as if my knees are going to give out. With a soft voice and tears in his eyes, he seems to look down to my very inner core, past the naked and vulnerable me that is shaking in her boots because she is touching Jesus. Ok, I know he isn't actually Jesus, but look at my baggage. Don't forget my baggage, people! We do not do this in Islam! Touching, dressing up like a prophet, ok Son of God, ok Jesus, whomever! We do not do this! I do not do this! But those eyes. They seem to know me, and I melt. He says to me, "I love you very, very much." And stands there with a smile, his warm hands have never let go of me. Touch someone else, touch someone else I keep thinking, go, talk to someone else in my group. Touch someone else! But he does not. He turns and hugs the little ballerina who leads him to his throne. And I am done.

Lights on, we move, I want to go home now. Where is Dewayne? I want to go home now! How do you get out of this place? Honestly, they twist and turn our group so many times through so many curtains and doors; I am not even sure how to exit this building that I have never been in before. But we move through to another room. The play seems to close, but I have no idea what was said there. I want to go home. I want out. I want out now! We move like sheep to the next room. Our guide has become almost a silent shepherd, who leads us from room to room. We are ever the obedient sheep who allow him to do it. "Not me," I thought. I start looking for exit signs.

New room, no scenery, just chairs. We all take a seat, and our shepherd leaves us. A man comes in and starts talking about what we have just seen. How there were three teens, who lost their lives that night. One chooses Jesus before her death, and she was the one I saw in heaven. But the other two were in hell. One because she rejected Jesus and one because she never made a commitment to make Jesus her Lord and Savior. She never prayed a prayer…and there it is. Almost like words that slurred into my land of, "I have no idea what you are talking about, people," Christian vocabulary words that I do not understand and are not explained. You might as well have been speaking to me in a foreign language because I could comprehend nothing. I hear him saying something about making a decision and would anyone like to talk to a counselor. And I remember thinking, "You people are the ones that need a counselor! You have a devil in the basement, stinky candles, ballerinas, and a guy dressed up as Jesus!" I hear him say, "Bow your heads and let's pray!" Praise the Lord! Well, honestly I don't know what I actually said, maybe praise something, but I know that is my opportunity to bolt. I know how these Christians work! They bow their heads and close their eyes, and I am given the opportunity to sneak out of there like those green and white judges who sit at the front of the room during Sunday service each week. So I move toward the door. Ten feet. Five feet. Almost there. Out!

   I am out. I blow past a desk with a lady and papers, past a room full of tables and chairs with people talking to other people. I hit the door fast! I mean I hit the door like a ton of bricks and then it opens. I want out! Past the tent, through the dark and cold, I find my way to my car. Hands still shaking, I try to get my keys from my pocket to unlock my car. I drop them, bend, and pick them up. My mind is racing, replaying voices that I have just heard. Still shaking, I am trying to get cold shaking hands to single out the car key. Ugh. Dang it! Dropped it again. Bend, pick it up, another try. I hear the last words the man says as I hit the door, "If you were to die in a car accident on the way home tonight, do you know where you will be spending eternity? In heaven or in hell?" Dang it! Dropped those suckers again. Now I bend, shaking, out of breath and cold. I bend, touch the keys, and see myself exhale. It is a very cold night. My breath is visible to me. I see the white of my breath against the darkness of the night, and it hits me. It hits me hard like a ton of bricks. I straighten up and answer the man's question. "Hell. I am going to hell."

Not exactly the answer I wanted. Not exactly the reply I wanted to give back. I get in the car, still seeing my breath. "Let everything that has breathe Praise the Lord." What? Where did that come from? I am now crying because all week long I had been talking to God and asking Him if I get to go to heaven. I wanted to go to heaven! How did those people in my class know that they get to go to heaven? I sob all the way home. Yes, all week I had asked God the question, "I want to know if I get to go to heaven." The answer was no. I am sobbing because I got my answer tonight, but it is not what I wanted to hear.

Looking back I knew then that I knew the truth. Now I had to deal with the truth, and His Name is Jesus.

Jesus answered, "I am the way and the truth and the life. No one comes to the Father except through Me."

John 14:6 (NIV)

No Peace

I did not have a good week. I had no peace. I had absolutely no peace. I would cry when I was alone. I would cry when I looked at my children. I would cry and hurt inside down to my core. Hell. I was going to hell. I would say it over and over, and it still stung. "I want heaven," I would beg. I hurt so deep that I would silently cry out like the girl in the dark room with the candles. I was so her. I was going to church. I carried a Bible. I tried to read it. I totally did not understand it. Most of the time I could not figure out what it said, but I was trying. I was a good person. I was a good mom. My children were wonderful and clean, happy and fed. I had very little, and I gave everything to them. They were my world, and they were so good and wonderful. How could this be possible? Hell!

I did not call my Sunday school teachers that week. I was still pretty mad at Dewayne for abandoning me that night. I did not call them because I had no more questions. I had an answer. Hell. And deep down, way down deep to my inner core, I knew it was true. I knew that I was going to hell, and I was not ok with that. I had no peace, but I held the truth in my hands. Hell.

The next Sunday morning rolls around. I drag my hell-bound self out of the house to "shop." I head off to church with a heavy heart and no peace. It is November 5th, 1995. I park the car and walk a honkin' mile up past the three trees. Here come the old white guys. I push past them and sit myself down this time. I even sit down before everyone else. They are still standing. I have yet to get to church on time. Slumped in the back pew, I have absolutely no idea what he is preaching on today. I am mad at God. Hell. That's not good enough! Then I tune in to what the preacher is saying. He is talking about decisions, too. Asking folks in the room if they have any decisions to make, or if they want to talk to someone. One by one I watch as people go up front. Someone greeted them, and they are taken out the side door. A couple goes up. Music is playing in the background, and people are praying. It's taking forever. Let's get on with this. I have a bone to pick with Dewayne I thought.

More go down only to be led away. Then I hear the pastor say, anyone else? Is there one more person who is sitting in the pew today that needs to make a decision that needs to come down front?" Me! Me! Me! Everything inside of me is screaming "Me!" but my feet are frozen. I want to, but I am too scared to move. Not a muscle moves, and he asks again. Go down front, and what, be lead out of the room like those other people? I've been to lots of Sunday morning services by this point. I have seen people be led out of the room before, and they never, ever come back. Even those green and white robe people never come back into the room. They all just disappear. God only knows what happens to them! You people sing about blood and have devils in the basement! I am going nowhere with you!

I feel a tap on my shoulder. It is a really tall white guy. He smiles and asks if I need to talk. I do not even know if I actually said yes out loud, but I let him lead me out of the back of the room. We go around the corner to another small room. It seems these buildings are nothing but small rooms! We sit in chairs directly across from each other. He introduces himself, and I tell him my name. He starts by saying, God told me to come over and talk to you. He said you have lots of questions that need to be answered today. Yes, and then the dam of tears and questions breaks forth. In the pile of mush that is me, I dump a thousand questions at this poor man of God; a sent one that did not know what God was throwing at him that morning, but he was obedient and talked to me. I have no idea how long we talked, but he never rushed me. He did answer everything I threw at him, and, somehow, I know down deep to my inner being that he is answering in truth.

I bow my head and close my eyes and pray the sinner's prayer. Hello, did you notice! I *bowed* my head and *closed* my eyes! I confess that I am a sinner, that I know that I have done wrong and that I am going to hell. I say that I believe that Jesus died on the cross for me to pay for my sins and rose from the dead to make a way for a sinner like me who is unholy to live out eternity in heaven with a Holy God, "Who loves me very, very much." I repent of who I am and ask Jesus to come into my heart and into my life to be my Lord and Savior.

He explains baptism to me and asks if I would like to be baptized. Wait, what? He explains everything. You know, being late to service week after week after week, I have never seen the start of the service, and I have never seen a baptism. He set me straight on the start time of the service and gives me a personal lesson on baptism. I agree to be baptized that evening at the start of the evening service.

Looking back I don't even know if I fully understood every word that I was saying, but I did know that I was hell bound, and that Jesus did love me, and that He wanted me to be with Him forever. I took a major leap of faith that morning. No, I had not totally figured out the Trinity or how Jesus was the Son of God. Nor was I sure of why His blood was so important or even what it meant for Him to be my Lord and Savior. But isn't that what a step of faith is? A leap of faith believes that something is there even when you can't see it. So I did my best Indiana Jones impression and stepped out onto that invisible rock bridge. I moved toward Him. I changed directions from the way I was going to His way. There were no fireworks or angels singing, but there was peace. There was peace so thick you could see it and touch it and definitely feel it. I was at peace. I belonged to Jesus! I was going to be baptized that evening! And, wow, I had no idea we had an evening service!

"That if you confess with your mouth, "Jesus is Lord," and believe in your heart that God raised Him from the dead, you will be saved. For it is with your heart that you believe and are justified, and it is with your mouth that you confess and are saved. As the Scripture says, "Anyone who trusts in Him will never be put to shame. For there is no difference between Jew and Gentile (non-Jewish person)-the same Lord is Lord of all and richly blesses all who call on Him, for, "Everyone who calls on the name of the Lord will be saved."

Romans 10:9-13 (NIV)

Know Peace

Now I am shopping twice today. I bid my children and parents goodbye, fully aware that they have no idea where I am going or what I am doing. I head to my first evening service and to be baptized. Part of me is scared, yet there is such peace. The peace that is so heavy that it squished the scared part of me into silence. I go into the building where I meet pastor "big tall white guy" who takes me up, up, up a small set of back stairs. He hands me off to a nice elderly man who explains that he does not usually do evening baptism, and his wife is in the nursery and unable to be here to help tonight, so please excuse her absence. I keep thinking it is probably a good idea to hurry this baptism thing along before anyone finds out what I am about to do. The fewer people who know that I am here, the better!

White robe on, my feet are cold. I have no idea why I am so willing to get myself into these situations. But the nice older man motions me to follow him, and I get my feet wet. Part of me wants angels to start singing, does my letter come down from the sky saying I now get to go to heaven? Knees are wet, so far so good, I have not died yet. I know because I start to think how my Muslim, Persian father is going to kill me when he finds out. Ok, now I am really wet and moving forward toward a man I have never met before. I would later find out he was the one in charge of Judgment House, but I do not know that now. He pulls me forward in the water and positions me. I do not realize how high up this bathtub is nor that there is an audience. Just me and God are talking. "I can't believe I'm doing this." I agree to follow Jesus and then I am fully immersed. "Raised in new life," I hear when I come up. New life. I do not fully understand that part, again a huge leap of faith, but I know that my old life is no longer good enough. It destined me for hell, and that is no longer acceptable. I want the new life that includes Jesus and heaven and everything that comes with it.

Exiting the pool and off to the changing room, it is quiet. No angels, no violins, no paper falling from the sky, but there is peace. I know peace and His name is Jesus.

Down the stairs, I slip. Up a large long ramp with handrails and green carpet. Round the corner to a huge hallway that leads to the sanctuary. I am going to go on home but those doggone ushers get to me first. This one is familiar to me, he has attacked me before, and grabs on to me and pushes me in through those wooden main doors. The service has started. There are a lot fewer people tonight than this morning. There seems to be a spotlight of some sort on that group of people down front. They are all surrounded by light, and they have started to pray. They are on their knees. I have not seen that before either.

I slip into my pew. My habitual habit of a back pew even though there is plenty of room for me to sit between my pew and the people in the light. I am hiding because I am unsure of what to expect. This is my first evening service. Now I am cold. My long, thick black hair is wet. I didn't know to bring a hairdryer. While I sit there, the preacher's words blend into a mumble that I am hearing, but not understanding. I worry about how I am going to explain to my father that I got my hair wet while shopping. Maybe it is good to sit here a while I thought, at least my hair can dry a little. There is mumbling from the front, but also rumbling in my spirit.

No angels, no violins, no fireworks or letters of congratulations. I start to worry about what I have just done. It has been a very eventful day. In one day, I have said that I believe in Jesus in the morning and by 6 pm I have been baptized in His Name. I notice a man lean up against the wall. He is leaning like the pictures of the Marlboro man on the billboards. Gentle yet strong, he is comfortable there, but he is not in the light with the rest of them. He and I are the only ones in the shadows at the back of the room. I am still talking to God. Panic comes. What have I done? Try explaining this one young lady. You think getting a divorce and being a single mother will bring shame on your family? Well, this one is going to take the cake.

I might as well dig my own grave extra deep because once they bury me, they will nail my coffin super tight to make sure I can't get out of the trouble I am in. I picture what that looks like in my mind, and I start after God. "God, how do I know that I've just done the right thing? How am I supposed to know if following Jesus is a good thing? There are no angels or violins, fireworks or paperwork! How am I supposed to know that I did a good job by accepting You as my Lord and Savior and getting baptized tonight? It's not like You have patted me on the back and said good job!" And I snap to because of movement. The Marlboro man is moving straight toward me with determination. Oh, Jesus! No, I should say like Jesus and the devil from the Judgment House play. Right to me! Directly with a purpose, full eye contact and all.

He leans in and whispers, "Young lady, did you just get baptized?" "Um, yes sir, yes sir I did." Part of me is thinking, hello, two and a half feet of wet black hair. Then he straightens up with a grin, and pats me on the back and says, "Good job," as he walks away. I don't know if it was seconds or minutes, but it might as well have been hours because when his words fully hit me, I froze in silence. "Good job." I had just sat there talking to God, which, by the way, is praying to God, as I have begun to figure out. It is not the repetitive set prayers of Islam that I had grown up learning in Arabic, but an authentic conversation with my Lord, my God. One in which sometimes I talk and sometimes I listen. Tonight I said, "Did I do the right thing?" I heard, "Good job." I even got a pat on the back.

Looking back that big tall white guy became one of my most favorite people on the planet. He knew the Lord and was obedient to His voice and stepped over to a very lost girl who could not even get the courage to step down an aisle to make a decision she knew she needed to make. And the very next Sunday I was on time to service. I even figured out what those green and white robe judges did, they sang, who knew? I also spent months after that night looking at the faces of all the tall men at church, trying to find the Marlboro man and I never did. Maybe he was my angel sent just to me, to reassure a very scared mess of a girl who was me, a former Muslim who had become a Christian that night. A girl whom God loves, "very, very much."

"We were therefore buried with Him through baptism into death in order that, just as Christ was raised from the dead through the glory of the Father, we too may live a new life."

Romans 6:4 (NIV)

Eyes To See And Ears To Hear

I received a wonderful gift on November 5th, of 1995. The gift of eternal life. But this gift is better than any gift that I have ever received before. It is the gift that just keeps giving. I also got a Savior who died for my sins. The Son of the Most High God died on the cross for me. He died on the cross for everyone else, too. I am learning that is a good thing. Sometimes death brings life. The old me had to die so that the new me could be reborn spiritually in Jesus.

"Therefore, if anyone is in Christ, he is a new creation; the old has gone and the new has come!"

2 Corinthians 5:17 (NIV)

"In reply Jesus declared, 'I tell you the truth, no one can see the kingdom of God unless he is born again.'"

John 3:3 (NIV)

Part of this wonderful gift is the Holy Spirit. The funny thing is, He and I have met before. I met Him before my car accident when I was warned about the no safety belts. I am sure He was the voice before I was to get married saying, "Don't do it." I have not listened very well to that voice in the past, but I am determined to be open to Him in my future.

Another part of the gift is receiving "eyes to see and ears to hear." What does that mean you ask? Well, it means that by me inviting Jesus into my life, He becomes a part of me, and He helps me in many ways. One huge way is that suddenly the Holy Bible starts to make more sense. I understand more and falling asleep less. I want to read it all of the time. Even when I do not fully understand it, I read it, and, in time, by reading it, praying and listening, God reveals it's meaning to me through the Holy Spirit. I never knew something that I was taught in my past could be so wrong. I was taught that the Bible was corrupt and that it was that way because it had been translated so many times in so many versions. The funny thing is, now with my spirit eyes and spirit ears, this so-called corrupted book of Scripture has become ALIVE to me. It is absolutely amazing! I had paged through my mother's white one when I was a child, but it didn't make sense. I had read it in college, but it didn't make sense. I had even tried to read the Bible before my step of faith and praying my sinner's prayer, but now everything is different because I am different.

Do you remember me telling you about my heart condition? The doctors discovered it right before the birth of my first child. Well, God knew it was there all along, but I did not. I was clueless as to the actual state of my heart. But now, with help from my new gift, I have eyes to see and ears to hear, and I understand my heart condition more than ever before. My heart was full of sin, and its condition was going to lead to eternal death. That means forever, people! Now I am forgiven, my heart has been healed. Now my heart is God's heart. My heart belongs not to me and my selfishness, but to God and His selflessness. God the Father, Jesus the Son of God, and the Holy Spirit are One God. Each a part of a whole that is able to heal my heart from the inside out. My heart condition has changed from death to life. I get to live out eternity with God, and that means life. That means forever, people!

The Holy Bible is the Word of God given to us, His creations so that we can learn more about Him and what He has planned for us. I never knew it was more than just a book. Now I know and intimately understand.

"All Scripture is inspired by God and profitable for teaching, for reproof, for correction, for training in righteousness; so that the man of God may be adequate, equipped for every good work."

2 Timothy 3:16 (NASB)

How do I know? Because I have read it and I still read it! After I got saved and began my personal relationship with the Most High God, I started to read the Holy Bible. At first, everyone sent me to the New Testament, but that was hard for me. There was too much to learn that was so opposite everything I had been taught when I was growing up. Then one of my Sunday school teachers gave me some good advice. Start at the beginning in Genesis. Why I thought? But I obeyed. The beginning of the Bible contained somewhat familiar stories. I read a lot. I do have to admit that at first Genesis was hard to read. That is a pretty scandalous book, people! Some of the stuff in there was very uncomfortable to read! Why would you sleep with your father, Lot, or look at your dad, Noah, naked? Yuk. But I pressed on. Some of the differences started me on new sets of questions. An example is Abraham and Lots story. In Islam, Lot is a prophet of God and Abraham's relative. But not in the Bible. He is Abraham's relative, but not a prophet. Another story that amazed me with such differences was Noah's.

In the Koran, I had learned that Noah had three sons, and when the flood came and it was time to board the ark, two of the sons choose to obey their father, but one son did not make it aboard the ark. That story always made me so sad because I felt bad for Noah. How could God ask so much of Noah then allow one of the sons to perish? It seems like Noah could not go about the work of God if he were busy mourning the loss of the one son. But, in the Bible, all three sons along with their wives obey God and their father, Noah. All three sons live! What a huge difference! That meant Noah was not on the ark mourning the death of a son but rejoicing in that God saved his whole family. To me, that was a huge discovery. In time, with lots of reading, I started finding out a lot of things.

Do you remember my question about why Jesus' blood was so important? The best explanation for me came from reading the Old Testament from the beginning, because, by the time I got to Leviticus, I was familiar with the beginning stories and the Jewish people. In fact, I was very happy I was not Jewish. I remember thinking how does one become a good Jew? I could never keep all of those laws and commandments. It seemed so hard to have to remember all of my sins, and make sure that I did the right thing with the dove, or the grain, or the other kinds of offerings. It's so much to remember. I lied about shopping when I was actually going to church. Is that dove or grain worthy? I was so relieved that Jesus paid for all of my sins, and that I did not have to try to fulfill all of those commandments. Then, in Chapter 17 of Leviticus, there it was, another answer to one of my oldest questions.

"For the life of the flesh is in the blood, and I have given it to you on the altar to make atonement for your souls; for it is the blood by reason of the life that makes atonement."

Leviticus 17:11 (NASB)

There it is! One of those Christian vocabulary words was finally explained to me. Atonement means to make reparation for a wrong or injury. Atonement means reconciliation. I, the unholy, have been reconciled with a Holy God by Jesus. Jesus was my blood atonement for my sinful life. Amazing!

As I was reading the New Testament, 2 Corinthians to be exact, I about fell out of my chair. Right there, in the eleventh chapter was a colossal passage! Don't forget what faith I was raised in.

"And no wonder, for Satan himself masquerades as an angel of light. It is not surprising, then, if his servants masquerade as servants of righteousness. Their end will be what their actions deserve."

2 Corinthians 11:14-15 (NIV)

One of the most basic Muslim teachings is that the prophet was given the holy book in a cave by an angel of light. What more could I say, or write, for God's Word is the truth, and He has clearly described what a lie I have been rescued out of. *Thank you, Jesus! Yes, I am specific now. Jesus, Jesus, and more Jesus!*

I could go on and on, but I want to leave you with this. As I studied and read, I began to let go of all of my old teachings, some slowly and some quickly. But one night there came a moment. I had been challenged by my parents on what I had been learning. Yes, they did figure out I was not shopping. Well, actually I told them what was going on. I did confess, and repentant of my evil shopping ways. It was part of the new me that wanted so much to be clean and at peace that I was willing to risk upsetting them greatly. The problem was that I was still in the learning stage, still the ever-absorbent sponge of information. Although I was reading the Bible, I had yet to grasp it as a two-edged sword to wage spiritual battle with my father. So one night he challenged me and my new book, and I was unprepared for battle. I sulked away like a spanked child.

Off in my room, I began to pray. God, what was that? I asked. Why didn't you burst in and defend me? Hello, are you listening? I know you are there. You are everywhere, so why didn't you help me out with that battle. I really could have used the help! So I settled down and began to think. I was determined to prove this Bible was indeed Holy and God inspired, and that my former book was not. So I went off to the bookshelf, grabbed a copy of the Muslim holy book and set it next to my Holy Bible on the table. I then began to pray something like this. "God, I'm sorry I doubted You, but I really could have used the help. I know that the name Mohammad and the word Islam are not in the Holy Bible because I have looked for it. But I need something from You. I need to know, intimately know and understand, that I am doing the right thing. That I am supposed to be reading this book and following it and not the other one. I need to know which book has the truth in it. Please, God, help me now."

So I opened my eyes to see both books sitting on the table in front of me. I started with the one that I no longer read. I closed my eyes, fingered the pages, and prayed that where ever my finger landed, God would give me my answer if it was truth. So I fingered a page, picked a spot, and opened my eyes. I read the verses, but they did not make sense to me. It was as if Aalia had written it in her jibber jabber language. In fact, it was so confusing that I read both pages that I had opened up to from top to bottom. I searched trying to make sense of what I was reading. Nothing.

I put that book down and picked up my Holy Bible. I did the same thing; I asked God to show me the truth. Eyes closed I fingered a spot to open the book, place my finger firmly at a point on the page and opened my eyes. The only problem was that as I read my eyes filled with tears…and truth. I had pointed to Isaiah 3:18.

"In that day the Lord will take away the beauty of their anklets, headbands, crescent ornaments, dangling earrings, bracelets, veils, headdresses, ankle chains, sashes, perfume boxes, amulets, finger rings, nose rings, festal robes, outer tunics, cloaks, money purses, hand mirrors, undergarments, turbans and veils."

Isaiah 3:18-23 (NASB)

I may have pointed to Isaiah 3:18, but God Himself pointed me to the truth. His Truth. The Bible is the Word of the Most High God. It is true in every way shape and form, and I believe it with everything in me down to my inner-most being. I knew that the words and names that I was looking for were not in the Bible because I had already been looking for them.

Looking back I was looking for a connection or common ground, so to speak. What I found was a picture in Isaiah of the very image of my people and me. Those few verses described my ancestors and me perfectly. In fact, I owned every bit of the clothing and items on that list that was for the females. I too had worn a crescent necklace around my neck for many years. But no longer. I was a new creation. I had been changed by the Truth, and the Truth has set me free.

"So Jesus was saying to those Jews who believed in Him, "If you continue in My word, then you are truly disciples of Mine; and you will know the truth, and the truth will make you free."

John 8:31-32 (NASB)

The Year Of The Sponge

I became a sponge. I soaked up anything and everything pertaining to Jesus that I could get my hands on. I read books that my teachers gave me on Sunday, and before the next Sunday, I would finish them so I could bring them back to them and get more. After I had exhausted their libraries, they introduced me to the library at the church. What a wonderful library! I loved being able to have access to new books about God. My world was opening up as fast as the past had been suddenly closed. It was a glorious time filled with everything bright, new, and green. I was a baby, growing, and eating as much as my Father God could provide. Oh wait, sounds like Adam came by his hunger honestly. He was a lot like his mother who was quickly looking a lot more like her Heavenly Father with each passing day.

I began to take my children to church. They just loved their Mr. Bob and Mrs. Tammy. Another part of that lovely gift from God on November 5th was trust. I began to trust people again. I found out that this church was not a cult, but a building full of people who shared Jesus with me.

I am welcomed into the family complete with a welcome new member's dinner, my first meal at the church. I am so excited. A plate is served to me and well, I do have to pause. I'm really not sure what it is. So I ask. It is pork wrapped with bacon, green beans cooked in bacon, and a few other items, but by now all I hear is pig, pig, and more pig. The cook must have sensed my fears or God Himself prompted him, but he quickly takes my plate, disappears, and brings me back some chicken. Mr. Mike became a forever friend that night. He saved me from me. He saved me from eating pig. I have accepted Jesus as Lord and Savior. I am reading my Bible, and I have even begun to take my children to church. But I am not ready for pork. Muslims do not eat pork. I do not eat pork. I am not ready to break down that wall yet. I am not ready for the other white meat!

I learn more and more new things. Some things simply become clear. Don't forget; I was an outsider who knew nothing of the culture, vocabulary, and ways of the Christians. I did not know what the Lord's Supper was, what sanctification meant, or why some authors in the Bible only wrote one book while others authored many. Simple things like figuring out who the Apostles and Disciples were. That Peter was Simon and Paul was Saul, but not the other Saul in the days of Samuel. Discoveries like there were multiple people in the Bible named Mary, James, and John. Who knew?

As I grew in the Lord and grew in my trust of others, I grew in relationships with other believers as well. I started to meet new people and learn new words like comfort zones, mission trips, discipleship classes, and dirty Santa games during Christmas parties. Mission trips and discipleship classes I find out are good. Comfort zones and dirty Santa games are bad. Don't even get me started on Santa. He is on my list along with Dewayne. Well, I guess I should let Dewayne come off the list now that I am forgiven, and I should forgive others, too. But Santa stays. That's a whole other chapter.

Back to comfort zones. Boy, do folks use those words a lot. At first, it sounds good, like an area to stay in and be comfortable in, right? I want a comfort zone! But slowly, I figure out that it is a phrase used when a believer wants to make excuses not to do what God wants them to do. I will give you an example. Remember how my father and mother were so active in our mosque. Well, my brother and I grew up serving in that mosque at a young age. Now, I am older, and I want to serve again, only this time in Jesus' Name. I pray for a place for the Lord to send me to serve. Then one day my prayers are answered. He wants me to serve in the baptistery area. Perfect, I thought. I can hand out towels!

My first day of serving, I step out of my comfort zone that I had wanted so much, and I volunteer to help with the ladies that go through baptism. I go upstairs really early before the service start. I know what you are thinking about me and service start times, but I'm telling you, I am a new creation! On time, and now showing up early to serve! Hello, baby Christian growing and glowing! So, I am early, I prepare the room, help the ladies pick out robes to fit, and, yes, hand out towels. But then the really neat part happens. I get to be in the circle of people behind the scene when the pastor prays for these new believers. I watch them go into the water old and come out new. I remember wishing that I could provide angels, violins, fireworks, and letters of congratulations!

But then the tears come. One by one, I watch the men and women, boys and girls, old and young profess their faith in Christ Jesus and then they too are fully immersed and come up "raised in new life." The water reminds me of birth. I figure out my new zone. I am the neonatal nurse to the new baby Christians that come through this church every other Sunday when it is my turn to serve. So I cry, and I pray and ask the Lord to help me never get a comfort zone. I never want one. I also ask Him to remove me from this service if I ever get to a place where my heart hardens, and I am no longer brought to tears by the profession of new believers in Christ Jesus. I wash the robes and towels and prepare for next week knowing that there are lots of people out there who need Jesus.

At one point during that year, I had been challenged by the testimony of a girl in our Sunday school class. She was memorizing Scripture, and she shared how she was doing it. It sounded so hard to me. Memorizing is so hard, I thought. I am not that smart. So I make excuses, and I realize that I am starting to form something called a comfort zone again. This comfort zone is called, "No Memorizing!" The task is too hard. I am a mother of two wonderful little ones who keep me so busy. The girl child is just like her mother in that she can talk 90 miles an hour and has a love for music. The boy child is just like his mother in that he asks 90 million questions a day, which I usually try to answer, but some questions he asks over and over and over. Those questions, the repetitive ones, I answer by saying, "Now Adam I already told you that one."

So I excuse myself of the hard task of memorizing the Bible, over and over, but everywhere I turn I am being smacked upside the head with it. So I ask God, "Why do I need to memorize Scripture?" Someone told me that God answers prayers one of three ways. He answers: "Yes, no, or wait." I beg to differ with them. I think He answers: "Yes, no, wait, and Shahe, I have already told you that one." So my last attempt at not obeying is that the verses are too long and hard to do. Then that God slap happens. Ouch! Upside the back of my head with a Holy Spirit reprimand of "You memorized lots of chapters in that other book, entire chapters, and in Arabic, and you can still say every single one. So why can't you memorize the Truth?" Ugh. I start memorizing that night. I am now officially out of my comfort zone!

Looking back I think I get my parenting skills from my Father God. One of my first verses, "Nothing is impossible with God." Luke 1:37 (Including memorization!)

"Nothing is impossible with God."

Luke 1:37 (NIV)

Starving Children In Africa

What's the worst thing you can do as a new believer? I think to share your faith in Jesus with someone who is totally against your faith in Jesus. What's the best thing you can do as a new believer? I wholeheartedly believe, share your faith in Jesus with someone who is totally against your faith in Jesus. Let me explain. I was still learning, and I knew that I did not have all of the answers, but I also knew that I had eternal life and that my family members did not. So I desperately wanted to share the beautiful gift of what I had been given with the ones that I deeply loved.

So I began with my mom. I shared verses with her. I read short devotions to her. I even tried to get her to come to church with me, but I usually failed. The harder I tried to make something happen, the harder she fought back with me. Each time she would blurt out a question or statement; sometimes I would know how to answer and sometimes I would not. Lots of our arguments ended with her questioning, "If God loves everyone so much, then why are their starving children in Africa?" Ugh, I didn't know that one! Africa. I would go to my Bible and look up every reference to "Africa." Nothing. Then I started searching books and consulting teachers. I even asked people and pastors at my church. I did not get a good answer, but I did get lots of funny looks.

But my mother was very open to reading any book, just, not the Bible. She especially loved reading books to her two grandchildren. Pretty soon I picked up on that, and I started to hide the common books with characters and colors, and I purposely put out books based on the Bible. She would tell the kids to go pick out a book, and they would bring her a toddler Bible or a book for example, on Noah. She would push it aside and say, "Don't you have a different book?" "Nope," they would reply, demanding, in their cute little brown ways, that she read the book they had brought. Grandma would cave and read them their books.

But, I also realized, that I was not going to be able to do this on my own. Not only would she eventually figure out where I had put all of the other books, but she would continue to ask hard questions that I was not prepared to answer. So I studied and then I started to pray. "Lord I need Your help! How can I answer a question that I did not know or even fully understand myself? I want my mom to go to heaven too; please help me Lord, I really need you!"

So I continued to look for new ways to share with her what I was reading and learning about God, Jesus, and the Holy Spirit. Our arguments would escalate. One evening she was in the kitchen, and I had evidently really stepped on her toes. She just let me have it complete with ending the argument with a G-D cuss word. I stood there and slapped her for cursing the Lord. It wasn't a hard slap, but it took us both by surprise. I had never slapped anyone before, and I am not so sure where that came from. I said I was sorry but told her to please stop cussing out God, and I ran upstairs crying. On my way up I remember telling God, "She's all yours, I have had it with her."

I stopped sharing with her, but I never stopped praying for her. I also continued to pray for an answer to that Great Wall of China question that she seemed stuck on. "If God loves all of us, then why are their starving children in Africa?"

Then one day I am driving home from somewhere. I always turn on Christian radio or listen to someone's teachings. This particular day someone from a popular program is teaching on family matters and parenting your children. Callers call in and ask questions and the experts on the radio answer. This day a parent is asking about a problem with a child, and then it happens. The expert stops his parenting advice mid-sentence and says, "Wait, I'm sorry, I have to stop and, well, you won't understand this, but I need to help someone else right now. I need to help them understand why there are starving children in Africa." Screech!

I pull my car off in a huff and a puff and stop, put it in park, turn up the radio, grab a pen at that same time, and write on the first thing I can grab. The man continues. "I'm so sorry to stop right now, but the Holy Spirit is telling me that I need to help someone understand why God loves us and why there are starving children in Africa." Ah! I'm ready Lord! He goes on, "There are starving children in Africa because man is sinful. A loving God who loves all of His creations has created a world in which we grow enough food to feed everyone on this planet. But mankind gets involved, and man is sinful. Man puts a monetary value on food. Man creates the situation where some have, and some have not. Man's sinfulness lets food rot on docks, and not get to those in need. Sinful man withholds food from the needy while paying for luxury $100 meals for themselves. Man's sinfulness causes him to keep for himself and not share with another. Sinful mankind makes one political group control another. And on and on." Then he stops suddenly and apologizes for getting off on a bunny trail and ends before the break with a prayerful thought that he hopes this helps someone out there listening.

You think! I am crying. Barely able to scribble fast enough and to see what I wrote, but there it was in wet blue ink, an answered prayer. A wall breaker. Thank you, Jesus! I start the car back up, get on the road, and head for home and my mom. Should I start an argument I thought, that way she can end it with her usual question and I can triumphantly blurt out the answer, or should I do something else? I think of a million ways to bring this up in conversation. But when I get home, none of them come to mind.

It is much easier than I think. I go into the kitchen; we talk a bit, and I bring up that God has answered one of my prayers on the way home today. She asks which prayer and I tell her that I had been praying for her and about her question about the starving children in Africa. Now I have her full attention. She listens to the whole explanation. It isn't the big wall crashing down noise that I am expecting. I was expecting something like what I imagined the wall of Jericho crashing down would have sounded. It is very silent. Nothing. She has nothing. She says nothing. She just takes it all in. The truth is said, she is soaking it up, and her processing is beginning. The Truth is beginning the process of setting her free too.

Looking back, I wanted to make or figure out the answer to her Great Wall of China question about the starving children in Africa. I guess I thought there might be a similar story in the Bible or maybe they didn't have the fishes and the loaves. Either way, God needed me not to handle this myself, but to give it to Him, so that I could learn more about the power of prayer, and my mother could get the answer to her question that kept a great big wall between her and the Most High God.

"For all have sinned and fall short of the glory of God."

Romans 3:23 (NIV)

Shovels Vs. Spoons

Shovels are hand tools. They are used for lifting, digging, and moving bulk materials. If you live in the north, you shovel snow. If you live in the south, you shovel red clay. But, if you are now a baby Christian like me, you shovel mud. Mud. I think that there are two different kinds of mud. One kind of mud is what you get yourself into before you were saved by Christ Jesus. That kind of mud is of your own doing. You are where you are because of yourself and the decisions you have made. You are dirty, and now that you are in the mud, everyone else can see that you are dirty too. I look at this kind of mud like this: M stands for "Middle." U stands for "Undecided" and D stands for "no Decision." This is the kind of mud you are wearing when you do not have Jesus. You are wearing mud because you try to have your sin and your cake too. You are on the fence, in the middle and do not want to commit one way or another. You are wearing mud because you are wearing flesh. You are undecided as to following Jesus, and that leads to mud that means you have made no decision for your eternity. Mud is a dirty thing.

Now there is another kind of mud. The one you are in after you are saved. Yes, we are back to pigs. Don't forget I was just like that Prodigal Son in the Book of Luke. I wasted my inheritance, and I have landed in the pig pen. But the pig pen has mud and this mud is not good enough. So I have run home to my Father God, and He has most lovingly welcomed me home with forgiveness and even new clothes. But I still have some mud on me. This kind of mud is forgiven mud. This kind of mud is of your own doing, but God is going to make a way where there is no way. You are where you are because of yourself, but you are not alone. God is with you. And the decisions you have made have still been made by you, but God will help you come out of those decisions in a way that brings Him glory. Forgiven mud is still dirty, it can still be seen by others including God, but God chooses to look past it because you have been forgiven by what Jesus did on the cross. His spectacular act of cleansing us free from sin did wash away my sins, but I still have to deal with the consequences of my sins-my mud. I want to wash the old mud off of me because even though it has been forgiven, I still have to deal with it, and God promises to help me do it. I really don't want to get my new clothes dirty with my mud. So I pick up two different tools.

A baby Christian uses a shovel to dig out their mud, lift it out of their lives, and move it away from where they are so that it no longer keeps them bogged down. In the beginning, I have a lot to shovel. Let me share with you a shovel-full. When I get angry, I use bad language. When I am frustrated, I use bad language. Even when I stub my toe, 99% of the time, I will use bad language. I come from a long line of bad language users. I can even swear in multiple languages. But that is nothing to brag about, not anymore because I have changed. God has changed me. So, as I am studying the Bible, I come across Luke 6:45.

"The good man out of the good treasure of his heart brings forth what is good; and the evil man out of the evil treasure brings forth what is evil; for his mouth speaks from that which fills his heart."

Luke 6:45 (NASB)

So I get out my shovel and start digging. It is not always easy. First, I have to control my anger. No more bad language. I keep shoveling. Then I have to control my frustrations. No more bad language. I keep shoveling. Shoveling is not easy, and I get tired. I lapse back into using bad language, but my new heart is pricked, and I do not like the mud on my new clothes. So I keep shoveling. Now when I stub my toe, my prayer is that I say, "Sugar nuts and corn flakes." Now, it sounds a lot more fun to shovel sugar nuts and corn flakes than the mud I was spewing!

Spoons are hand tools too, only smaller in size. Sometimes the amount of mud that I need to remove seems small to me. Let me share a spoon-full with you. My sweet southern Granny had trouble with my ex-husband's Middle Eastern name. She and I were talking about my circumstances. In her frustration, she called him "Butthead" instead of using his name. Sounded good to me. So we adopted that name from that point forward. It gave me a sense of power, and although I felt mean saying it, I will admit it also satisfied me. I liked not saying his name. I liked "Butthead." And it was just once in a while when I was frustrated or angry. No big deal I thought. And at the time we started doing this, my children were very young, and we never did it around them. I was sneaky in my mud.

I am reading about blessings and curses in Scripture. The Lord is teaching me to pray blessings over my children and circumstances, and because it is a good thing, I feel good about myself. But my prayers of blessings are not working. So I ask God why. He quickly convicts me of my mouth.

"A wise man's heart guides his mouth, and his lips promote instruction. Pleasant words are a honeycomb, sweet to the soul and healing to the bones."

Proverbs 16: 23-24 (NIV)

My mouth is saying butthead. I am so sad and ashamed when I realize that my dirty mouth meant that my heart is dirty too. It has mud all over it again.

So I get out my spoon and use it to dig out my yuk, lift it out of me by prayer, and throw it behind me never again to be in my heart. That is a very big spoon-full. I also feel convicted to make others stop saying it. Spoons work. Spoonfuls of honeycomb and blessings are even better. Prayers work because my blessings begin to happen when my curses begin to stop. God is good, and my forgiven, saved heart is in the process of being cleaned out of my mud. Sometimes the quantity is so large that it takes a shovel. Sometimes it seems insignificant and small, so I use a spoon. Either way, it matters to God. I matter to God. To use big churchy terms, I am being sanctified, purified, and set apart.

Looking back I realize that my shovels and spoons were gifts from God. Sometimes they looked like the Word of God, other times the Holy Spirit, and still other times the face of God Himself. God gives us the tools of prayer and reading our Bible to help us garden in our heart with the ultimate Helper Himself, the Holy Spirit. The best part is when you have worked in the garden together for a long while, and He says, "You are done, come over beloved, and let's wash the mud off of you."

"Whoever gives heed to instruction prospers, and blessed is he who trusts in the Lord."

Proverbs 16:20 (NIV)

I Have Decided To Follow Jesus

Spring is here. Flowers are in full bloom, and I find myself in love with the south and my Jesus. Soft breezes and stroller rides with my children. Puppies and swings, butterflies and trips to Granny's mountain. The kids are growing up quickly, and Aalia will start kindergarten in the fall. Time seems to pass so fast. We are attending church regularly. They love church, Sunday school, and Bible stories. They get to have a snack and play outside. They even make art projects. Why is it that their art project is always wet glue and blue paint, with lots of colored sand and glitter?

It is May and Mother's Day. We take our place in the pews before the service begins. Adam slides down my lap to quietly play with his toy car at my feet. He usually spends most of the service under the pew in front of me. Aalia sits beside me with her pen and paper. She takes sermon notes like me only without words. She listens intently and every once in a while pops up with a hard question. Mommy, why did Jesus *have to* die on the cross? Mommy, if God loves us so much then why did He make Satan? Mommy, will I see my puppy in heaven? Mommy, why does the preacher say this or that. She is her mother's daughter in that she asks too many questions too!

But this Mother's Day is different. Today she doesn't ask questions but sits there quietly. She doesn't write anything down, and at the end of the service she turns to me and announces that she wants Jesus in her heart too. No, she is not discussing this, or even questioning it. She, at five years old, turns and says, "Mommy I want to make Jesus my Lord and Savior." I say, "Ok, honey, we will talk about it in a few moments." You see I was an adult who took ten years to get from a youth group conviction that I needed Jesus until I prayed to invite Jesus into my life. I thought, what could this little one possibly know about asking Jesus into her heart? She is five! I turn to my friend and ask her if a child can make a decision for Jesus at such a young age, but as I turn back, there she goes.

That little girl in a red dress and ruffles marches down that aisle all by herself without me. She knows what she wants. She knows who she wants. She isn't afraid like her mother and goes right down the middle aisle. She goes right up to the pastor and announces it for all to hear. I'm still in the back of the church, frantic, afraid as a saved person to go down that big aisle. What about Adam? Would I have to peel him out from under the pew and off of the floor? There she goes. They've taken my baby girl through the side double doors. Gone, forever! I exit out the back with cars, papers, Bibles, and the boy in search of my little girl.

Finding her in a room talking to the pastor, I slide in to listen. He asks her questions that she has actual answers for. He asks her does she understand sin. Yes, she explains, "It is when you do something wrong, and it makes God sad." He asks her if she sins. "Yes, every day, and sometimes," she says, "I even get in trouble for it." He asks her why chose Jesus. She says, "Because He is the only one that God has chosen to be His perfect Son and He is the only one you can choose to get to live with God forever." The confidence in this child is amazing. I am in awe of her answers. I am in awe of the God in her because of her age. I am in awe of how young her journey will start compared to mine. He asks her more questions, and she answers. Then she says, "Can I please just invite Him into my heart now. I need to do this today." Heaven forbid we prevent a little one from getting to Jesus! So the pastor leads her in the sinner's prayer. She is ever so pleased that she has Jesus in her heart and wants to get bap-pi-tized-did as soon as possible to show Jesus she is His. Who is this kid?

Looking back, she is the child of the Most High God. She is the one who heard the call at a young age and followed His voice without question. She is the little girl that was not held back by traditions or culture, limits and boundaries that our adult selves place onto ourselves. She was a clean slate waiting for Jesus to write His Name on her heart. She was the baby girl that gave her mother the greatest Mother's Day gift a mother could ever ask for. She was bap-pi-tized-did in June by the Texas pastor, after going through the New Christian's Class at church. A precious woman named Mama Lou taught the class, and she assured me that she was ready and that it was real. May it always be so, that my daughter surpass me in my walk with the Lord so that she can spend as much time with Him in this life time as possible!

"Then little children were brought to Jesus for Him to place His hands on them and pray for them. But the disciples rebuked those who brought them. Jesus said, "Let the little children come to Me, and do not hinder them, for the kingdom of heaven belongs to such as these."

Matthew 19:13-14 (NIV)

Welcome To Spiritual Warfare

It's July, and he's back. It was supposed to be a one-week vacation in the summer to visit with the children who are now three and five. Now it is two weeks. He is talking about getting back together again. I am thinking, "Will this vacation ever end?" Two weeks have now passed. Go away, go north, and go home. We have been divorced and living in different states for three years. He in the north and I in the south. I like it here. I like the flowers and the trees, the easy winters, and the distance from him. I like my new life in Christ Jesus. Right now, except my parents, no person here knows who I used to be. I have freedom in my new life because no person here knows the old me. But that all changes quickly when he announces that he is moving here. Everything changes!

I go and talk to a minister at the church. He is in charge of the counseling ministry. I am not afraid of the word "counseling" anymore. I have a new term that scares me. It is "benevolence." I have no idea what that is, but it has its own ministry. Back to getting some counseling. I go and talk with him. In a heavy Texas accent he declares, "Well honey, welcome to spiritual warfare!" I have no idea what he is talking about, but can't you just smell the sweet tea on his breath? I come away from that meeting with a new appreciation for what God has already shown me and what He is about to show me.

Looking back a battle was brewing, and it was bigger than a batch of sweet tea! My year of the sponge was on hyperdrive because God knew I was about to be at war. Not with the ex, he was just the earthly example. It was with the powers that I cannot see. Chains were being broken. Captives were being set free. Generational curses were being lifted. Walls were coming down. Stones were being overturned. I was learning to put on my battle suit for spiritual warfare. My new clothes of salvation have a new layer. It's battle armor. It's the Armor of God.

"Finally, be strong in the Lord and in His mighty power. Put on the full armor of God so that you can take your stand

against the devil's schemes. For our struggle is not against flesh and blood, but against the rulers, against the authorities, against the powers of this dark world and against the spiritual forces of evil in the heavenly realms. Therefore put on the full armor of God, so that when the day of evil comes, you may be able to stand your ground, and after you have done everything, to stand. Stand firm then, with the belt of truth buckled around your waist, with the breastplate of righteousness in place, and with your feet fitted with the readiness that comes from the gospel of peace. In addition to all this, take up the shield of faith, with which you can extinguish all the flaming arrows of the evil one. Take the helmet of salvation and the sword of the Spirit, which is the word of God. And pray in the Spirit on all occasions with all kinds of prayers and requests. With this in mind, be alert and always keep on praying for all the saints."

Ephesians 6: 10-18 (NIV)

School

During the summer, I had decided to homeschool my children. But then the enemy sent arrows at our home. Direct Hit! My parents separated. Their marriage was headed to divorce court. My father carried heavy burdens from my divorce, single parent status, shame, and conflict with family. Instead of choosing the family or me he just "checked out" and left. My mother was broken, and now I needed to get a job. Homeschool was no longer an option, but neither was a public school. I needed the kids to have a home, school, and church teaching Jesus. That way it wasn't mommy versus daddy, but Jesus versus no Jesus. So I got a job and an appointment with the local private school to find out about their homeschool umbrella group.

The elementary principal, Mrs. B., is a wonderful lady with a heart for Jesus. She gives me wonderful advice and suggests that the children should attend the school instead of homeschooling since I will be working. I tell her I have no idea how to pay for this, so she suggests that we pray. Her precious prayer asks the Lord for provision, and I feel such a peace about this school. Before I leave, she tells me to take the school years one-by-one, praying for monthly provision instead of worrying about the years to come. A godly, good word from a godly, good principal. I drive away and looking at the school's sign I get a sudden word from the Lord. A promise. My children will both graduate from this school one day. Graduate? But they haven't even started yet! I both laugh and cry! Fall is closing in, he is still here, and my daughter will start kindergarten at a local private Christian School.

Looking back I see a young mom trying to "make" things happen. I had a "to do" list and things needed to get done on that list. Get Aalia ready for kindergarten, get a job, take care of my mom, take care of my kids, lean on Jesus, lean on Jesus some more, and the list goes on. But what I plan "to do" and what God plans "to do" may be two very different lists. My list versus His list. If I am obedient to God, His list should win. If I am disobedient, my list gets checked off one by one, but I walk in disobedience. I am learning quickly that walking in disobedience is not a good thing "to do."

"Samuel said, "Has the Lord as much delight in burnt offerings and sacrifices as in obeying the voice of the Lord?" Behold, to obey is better than sacrifice, and to heed than the fat of rams."

1 Samuel 15:22 (NASB)

Burger King Vs The King Of Kings

Fall is here, and the school has started. She has been attending school for a few months now. Adam cries every time she goes to school. He wants a "pack pack" (backpack) and homework too. The boy cries for homework. I remind him that one day this will all change! So I enroll him in two days a week for preschool. He absolutely loves it. You should hear that sweet boy sing Scripture! He stands in the front of the room, taller than most of his classmates. *Did I mention he is huge?* And belts out Psalm 23, the whole thing. *Did I mention that I whine about memorizing Scripture?* This kid puts me to shame. He has learned so much in Ms. Melody's classroom! He has learned so much about Jesus from Ms. Melody! *Thank you, God, for Ms. Melody.*

Saturday rolls around, and it brings a trip to Burger King. They have a playground, and we can have supervised visitation in a public place. We order our meal and sit in the booth. I realize that I am wearing my cross necklace and decide to tuck it in my shirt, so he doesn't see. No need to cause friction and get him upset! I remind the three and five-year-old that they can play after they eat. I pass out the food, Adam has his usual "chicken, ketchup, and Sprite," as if ketchup is a food group. I guess it could be since he only ever licks the ketchup off of the French fries. The food is passed out, and their dad starts to eat. Aalia blurts out that he has to stop, we forgot to pray. That is something that we do all of the time now. We bow our heads; I am not sure if he did because I am pretty sure he is wondering what is going on at this point.

Aalia starts singing, "God our Father, God our Father..." He erupts, "What? God your Father? What is this, God is not your Father! What kind of prayer is that?" She waits. When he is done, she begins again. "God our Father, God our Father, once again..." Once again, he erupts. More fussing. Now she is not amused either. She is determined to make it through the whole song while he is still arguing. Then you hear Adam say, "AAAA men!" And the kids start to eat.

Oh my, I am dying. I had no idea this would happen, but I am praying to God in my head, my heart is racing. He calms down. Looking out the window he sees a flag; he asks her if she knows the Pledge of Allegiance. "Of course," she says, "I pledge allegiance, to the Christian flag of the..." "What, what is this? That is not the pledge! What kind of school do you go to?" Insert more fussing here. I explain that it is a Christian school. He says that I became a Christian just so they could go to that school. I am thinking, "Ha! He has no idea!"

Then he gets control and asks what she learned in school yesterday. A song she replies, "Would you like to hear it?" Sure, sure, sing me a song. "I have decided to follow Jesus; I have deci...." A volcanic eruption and now everyone in the room is looking at us. "What have you done?" He is angry and turning red, which, for a brown man, is hard, but evidently possible. By this point, I can't decide if I should laugh or cry. You can't help but see the humor in it all. She is just five! So he calms down and says, "No more Jesus! Sing me a song. Sing me a real song. Sing me a rock and roll song." Without missing a beat that little bugger broke out in the loudest, "Jesus is the rock that rolls my blues away, bop shoe bop whew," complete with hand motions and butt wiggles. Now all...everything breaks loose. The yelling, the accusations, the children are upset, so I pack up the chicken, ketchup, and sprite because we need to leave now.

Exiting the booth she puts her little hands on those five-year-old hips and looks up at her six-foot-two-inch tall daddy with those deep black eyes and tells him that if he didn't believe in Jesus that he was going to hell. All he heard is, "Daddy go to hell!" Ahhhh! In one scooping motion I gather kids, food, coats, crowns, drinks, toys from the meal, and head for the car. I keep smiling and thinking about how I was worried that he would see my cross necklace and get upset. Ha! I had no idea!

Looking back, well, honestly I can't help but laugh. It's one of my all-time favorite moments in life. Not the fighting part, or getting him upset part, but the God part. Can't you just see that brown baby girl in her littleness up against his brown man bigness! God was all over this. I can't help but wonder if He wasn't sitting on His throne laughing and just enjoying this child and her boldness for Him.

This memory also reminds me that God Himself pursues each of His creations. He speaks into our lives at every turn. He uses the Bible, people, trials, and tribulations. He uses something small like a song or big like the world around us that He has created. He uses prayers from an elderly principal and prayers from a young child. He uses everything to pursue us. He goes after us with all of His heart so that we will be transformed to have a heart like His. After all, He is the King of Kings!

"On His robe and on His thigh, He has this name written: "King of Kings and LORD of LORDS."

Revelation 19:16 (NIV)

The Mosque

Have you ever tried to make something happen? Have you ever tried to make something *not* happen? Well, I am still in the obedience stage. Still struggling, still wanting to be in control, and take care of things myself. But God has other plans, plans that include letting go and leaning on Him. Plans that include less of me and more of Him. So our recent revelation that I am a Christian and that I am taking the children to church has suddenly brought my ex to the realization that "he needs to raise his children in Islam." So he plans a trip to the local mosque. We have a local mosque? Who knew? I didn't. I moved south and never even looked for one, but low and behold, there is one, near downtown, and he wants to take the kids there.

He makes plans. I have no plans. I don't want his plans! We do not have any formal visitation arranged, no court papers, and no guidance. It's him versus me, but I have legal and custodial custody. I tell him, no, but he insists. So he makes a plan for Sunday. He is taking his kids to the mosque, and his parents are coming too. So, I do what I am learning to do. I go to God in prayer. I pray for vomit, I pray for illness, I pray for storms, car trouble, or death. I pray for natural disasters and personal ones. I beg and plead and pour my heart out to God, *"Please Lord, I'm not ready to hear Muslim prayers again. I'm not ready to expose my kids to all of this yet."* So like all good baby Christians, I pray and then do the opposite. I lean on my own understanding and my own ways and not His! I plan to pop tires or put sugar in the gas tank. I plan to expose the kids to major diseases like the chicken pox, but I can't find anyone with it! Why can't you get a chicken pox kid when you need one? I plan to do this or that, all the while arguing with God in my head. Fix this I demand. Fix this I demand some more. Why can't God just send a tornado to wreck the mosque before Sunday? Is that too much to ask the Most High God? You think that I say all this in jest, but I am seriously praying for body fluids and natural disasters, people!

Sunday rolls around, I wake up, and still no vomit. Great, perfectly healthy children, ugh! Thanks a lot, God! Great. He pulls up in his car, a perfectly running vehicle, ugh! Thanks a lot again, God! So we load the kids up in their car seats in my car, and I drive. I follow him and his parents in his car, and we head off to the mosque that I never knew existed, ugh! Thanks a lot, God! Are you listening up there? While driving, I am off and running my mouth to God. Arguing in my head, explaining to God why vomit or a popped tire would be a really good thing right now to make supernaturally happen. Call up some wind or something. Are You, not the boss of the universe? So, 90 mph my talk (prayer) goes to God. I just follow his car and continue to pray (talk) to God.

Great, we are here, ugh! We get out, unbuckle car seats, and I am still arguing with God. Diaper bag, sippy cup, auto mommy mode, and movement toward the front door. "Why have you not intervened, God? Where is my vomit, my stalled engine, and hurricane?" I walk through the front door, and my hurricane hits. I walk into the eye of the storm. In all of my arguing with God, I forgot a few simple key things. One, my head scarf. I have not worn one in a long while, and mine is around my neck and not on my head. Two, I walk into a mosque that I have never been to before. In all of my moaning and groaning, I forgot that men and women do NOT use the same door, and I have unknowingly walked head uncovered right through the men's door. Now, this mosque that I am so unfamiliar with was a converted building, you know, one that had been something else but it became a mosque. It was not made to be one originally, so the main men's door also happened to be at the very front of the prayer hall. Prayer halls have all the people praying toward Mecca in Saudi Arabia, so that means that every male eye in that room has just seen my naked, hair uncovered head walk right into the front door. I stand there at the front of the room. Wait for it…5, 4, 3, 2, 1. It was like a five-second silence then a verbal volcano of Arabic erupted. Blah, blah, blah (in Arabic of course) and getting louder.

I make only one or two steps through the door when all hell breaks loose. Yes, I said, "hell." I am not cursing, hell is a place, and we have just stepped into that place. Men get up in huge numbers and charge the front door. They do not recognize us; my ex has never been there before either. He is afraid too. He scoops up Aalia and puts her on his shoulder, and I grab up Adam, and we both get pushed backward by the crowd. I have no idea where his parents go, but we all go back outside and quickly. More yelling, more Arabic. Too fast, I can't keep up with my poor Arabic skills, and the crowd is large and loud. I am truly frightened. "Why have you brought your wife here?" He responds, "That's not my wife, we are divorced." More yelling. Now he is really afraid too.

He shoves Aalia into my car and I shove Adam. He tells me to get in and lock the door and this time I obey him. Yes, it can happen. Miracles I tell you! I am a changed woman and a scared one too! He shoves his mom into his car and then he and his dad start to diffuse the situation. I have no idea what they say because I stay in that car. I buckle the kids into their seats from the inside, get them settled in with sippy cups and little snacks, and I even start the engine. Don't fail me now car! Oh God please, please, please, don't answer that prayer now about the stalled car! After what seems like a lifetime, my ex comes to the car and tells me that this is the "men's building" and that we need to drive to the other building where the women and kids are. It's just down the street. So we start off again, great, ugh!

I follow him, and his parents in their car and the three of us are in our car. We make left turns and right turns, then right turns and more left turns. We drive around for more than an hour. No women's/children's building to be found and we are very lost. Finally, it is now almost three hours into this journey to the mosque and the kids have to use the restroom. This is before cell phones, so as soon as I see a McDonald's off in the distance, I honk my car horn and pull into the Mickey D's. He pulls off ahead and turns around. He's upset that I've stopped, but I explain that we are about to have some major accidents. I whisk the kids off to the restrooms and return to the wonderful smell of French fries. That's it. The kids declare the day over and run off to the play place while hollering out that they want "chicken, ketchup, and Sprite." "What? We are not playing, eating, or staying here," he declares. "Yes we are," his father declares, and we sit. Playgrounds, chicken nuggets, and Sprite trump any plans my ex has. They fetch the meals. I sit quietly with his mom. We are all spent, tired, bewildered, and hungry. I don't think that McDonald's has ever tasted as good as on that day!

We adults sit quietly and eat our meals. The kids play and bounce back to the table for a fry or a nugget, then back to the play area. Normally I would make them sit at the table and eat first and then play, but today is different. They have been through enough, and so have we. As I sit here watching their smiling faces and listening to their laughter, I find myself thanking God for them, and it hits me. It hits me hard. My prayer has been answered. It wasn't exactly what I said, vomit not included. But it is perfect. Ugh! God is so good.

Looking back I realized that my prayer was more than car trouble and body fluids. I tried to make something happen. I tried to make sickness and machinery fail so that I could succeed and not take my family to the mosque. I thought I had the short term answer. My way was messy but easy. But God had a better plan. His always are better and bigger than our littleness can comprehend. Not only did I pray for physical breakdowns in the body and in vehicles, but I also pleaded for help, "Please Lord, I'm not ready to hear Muslim prayers again. I'm not ready to expose my kids to all of this yet." Why do I love my God so much? Because His ways are not my ways and His plans are always bigger and better and long term. Not only did I not take more than a couple of steps into that door, but I also disrupted prayer time. The children and I NEVER heard a single word of prayer uttered. We never found the women's or children's building. We never participated in the old ways. Not only that, but God did one more really big thing. Wonder if He shows off a little from time to time? But because of the giant mess we caused and the fear that it caused, we never went back. The ex NEVER brought it up again. To this day my children and I have NEVER been there or to any mosque in the North, South, East or West. Yup, He is showing off. Guess I need to let go and let God get all of the glory He so deserves. After all, it was all Him; I was just the argumentative participant in His greater plan for all three of us!

"When a man's ways are pleasing to the LORD, he makes even his enemies live at peace with him." Proverbs 16:7 (NIV)

I Begin To Work At The Church

Never in my wildest dreams did I ever plan out my life in a way that it should look like it looks right now. (This still totally applies to my life!) I studied nutrition and psychology with the hopes of one day helping children with eating disorders. But since my divorce, I have worked as an assistant manager at a gas station, the express line at night in a huge chain store, and I have done home daycare. At this time my current situation am typing at home and watching two other little girls along with my two. When they nap, I type. When I put them down for the night, I type some more. But this ends with the increased use of computers. I type dictation reports from engineers. The computers are shutting that area down, and they offer me an office job. I take it, but it means giving up the home day care. I am about to discover the real world and the real worlds view of my faith in Jesus.

During lunch, I brown bag it, read my Bible, and kind of keep to myself. I like the quiet time. It is rare in my world. But others in the office take offense to it. They think that I am an elitist and made comments like, "she thinks she is better than us." I ignore them, but they did not ignore me. My supervisor even tells me that I cannot keep my Bible on my desk and that I have to put it in the drawer because I am offensive to others. I guess it is offensive just to her, because I continue to put the Bible there, and I did not get in trouble from anyone but her.

During the day shift, I worked. When it comes time to leave, I walk outside, greet my mother and children, exchange hugs, and she goes in to work there too. I take the kids home and play mommy for the rest of the evening. It works pretty well until the elevator day.

We work for the same insurance company on different shifts. Because we work on the same floor as the claims department, we have security badges to let us come and go through the main doors in the middle of the office building. The claims department often deals with disgruntled, angry people, so security is tight. One day I start to go downstairs when I notice someone behind me. As I approach the door, I suddenly feel very "not at peace," and I dive over to the water fountain. Drinking the water, I notice the person go through the door, but it never "clicks" as it should when again we are secure. My spirit is not calm.

I enter the middle elevator area lobby, and it is just a young man and me. He pushes the button, and we wait for the elevator. The door opens, and he steps in. I hear that voice, "Don't get in." I step one foot into the elevator, and just as the doors are closing, I step back in obedience to the voice, His voice. "I forgot something I comment," as the door shuts. Once he is gone so is my lack of peace. I know without a shadow of a doubt that I had just avoided danger. The other elevator opens, and I get in. Riding down I thank the Lord for His voice, teaching me obedience. It is the end of the workday. I have my Bible in a Bible carrier with a handle in one hand and my purse and lunch sack in the other hand.

My head is down in thought when the doors open in the lobby. There he is. He pushes me back into the elevator, swipes a card, the doors shut, and we go to the basement. He is all over me. He is grabbing and pulling at me, trying to touch stuff he shouldn't. I am so mad that I have let my guard down. What he didn't plan on is that the Lord is all over me. As he has me pinned up in the corner and I can't fight him off, I start praying. *Lord help me, I need you, what do I do, make him stop. My mouth is now speaking out loud. I continue. "They say that the Lord does not give you more than you can handle, and I can't handle this right now Lord."* I unleash on him all of the frustration of the past few years. This Persian goes, well, Persian.

That's when I hit him upside the head with my Bible bag. A good hit too because it not only surprises him, but he falls back a bit, and I am no longer pinned in the corner. I continued to say out loud, *"The Lord does not give you more than you and handle, and I can't handle you right now."* I also continue to beat him with my Bible. It is a full out punching and wrestling match in a locked elevator, and I hear the voice again. "Put your fingers in the crack, touch the gray area and the doors will open." With one leg kicking him away and one arm locked with his, I fall forward in one motion reaching with both hands to the center of the closed door. I pinch my fingers inside as he takes better hold of me and just as I am being pulled backward my fingers find the gray rubber that triggers the doors open. The doors open and there is a man in the basement waiting to go up who helps rescue me from the man in the elevator.

It is so upsetting because the man in the elevator is a co-worker. I go outside with both of my wrists throbbing and meet my mother with tears. I explain what happened, and she says that I need to tell management. She goes inside; I take the kids home. I call my boss from home and explain everything to her. I think it is handled. The next day I come in, and she calls me into her office. She tells me that she reprimanded him and that it is probably my fault for leading him on. What? I was so not expecting that. I return to my desk in tears. My wrists are swollen and sore, and typing is very difficult. It takes an hour before I get up the courage to tell her that how she handled it is not good enough. I return to my desk and call the corporate office. It takes off from there. They take my statement, send me to the doctor, and call my boss. My boss calls him back into her office and fires him. Again, I think that it is all handled. I return from the doctor with two severely strained wrists in wrist braces. My boss states that since I shouldn't type, and since she is short a worker in the mail room because she had to fire him today, that I should go in there and do his work.

For the next few weeks, I have to do his job. I work quietly in his area with his co-workers listening to them say things like, "wonder what happened," and, "what's he going to do for money, he just bought a new car." They did not know why he was fired, and I just want to crawl into a hole. It is so difficult in there. But this time, I changed whose authority I go to for help. Man's authority is not working. So I pray to God. He steps in and rescues me once again.

The next time I pull my car into the church, and as I still have my hands on the steering wheel, I feel the overwhelming promise of God that I am going to work here someday. Church? What in the world will I do at a church?

Looking back God answered my prayers prayed in that season, and He answered prayers I had yet to pray for the next season to come. God positioned me out of my miserable place to place me with people who would support and love me and even let me leave my Bible on my desk. He gave me godly bosses, and I felt beyond blessed to be so protected. What I didn't realize was how protected my next season needed to be.

"Since no man knows the future, who can tell him what is to come?"

Ecclesiastes 8:7 (NIV)

Court

Time is passing, and my children are growing. We are all growing in our relationship with the Lord. For years we have read the Bible at bedtime. It started with a child's version of the whole Bible. I would read a story a night and then several stories. We have read through this Bible multiple times, and now Aalia is reading it to me. She is a good reader, and they don't like to miss our Bible time. God is in their school, in their church, and in their home.

The ex-husband is not happy that the God of the Bible is in our lives in such a big way. He doesn't like that they go to a Christian school, but he attends their school programs and gets to hear Bible stories and Bible verses. He doesn't like that they go to a Christian church, but he attends their sports games and some church activities and gets to hear more from the Bible and about the Jesus in the verses. He doesn't like their home situation. He decides that is where he will fight back, so he starts the process to take me to court to fight over the children and their custody.

Now I am going to shorten the telling of this process which was many years into one chapter. Why? Because the details and the arguing, the paperwork filed and the money exchanged, even the process itself is actually very insignificant. What is important is to see God in all of it. I have started working at my church in the preschool and children's ministry. The children and I are surrounded by a body of believers that is like the Bible says, "a cloud of witnesses." We are loved on by God and His people, and we love it.

Now court comes. Quietly during prayer time, God reveals to me that, "I am not to fight the ex in man's court." Man's court? What in the world, I thought. But then I get papers. He is taking me to court for unsupervised visitation. I sell some jewelry to pay for an attorney. We go to court. What was supposed to be a visitation hearing turns into a full-blown court case. This "case" takes weeks, which turn into months and now years. Details, details, details. All kinds of flesh details are required, but God is showing Himself in the courtroom. Let me share with you just a couple of examples that played out in the courtroom.

He says he wants the kids during the Christmas vacation. Why I counter, you don't celebrate Christmas? He says I'll get them a tree and presents. The judge, he says he will get them a tree and presents. Me, it's not important to have a tree and presents, it's not about Santa. It's about Jesus and His birth and God's plan for us all through Jesus.

He wants them out of the kids' school. Why I counter, it's a good school? He says I'll pay for them to go to another school that is private, but not a Christian one. The judge, he says he will pay for their school. Me, it's not about "a private school," it is not important to have a private school. It's about a school that teaches them about Jesus.

Back and forth we went in court for over three years. Then two significant markers happen in this journey with the Lord. The first involved the children. The judge was so fed up with the argument of whether the kids should be raised as Muslims or as Christians that he asked to have them brought to court. This scared me because I had no idea of what was going to happen, and neither did my attorney. He was not a divorce attorney. I had been divorced for years. He was not a family attorney. He usually did not get involved in custody cases. He was an attorney that specialized in the rights of Christians. Again, this was a much bigger battle than the case our flesh eyes could see. It was a spiritual battle played out in a building made by man.

Now a side note. Adam is older now around three or four, and he rarely talks. Oh, he can talk, he just chooses not to. I had his hearing tested. I had him to multiple doctors. I even had folks at church praying for him to talk. But a very wise pediatrician examined him and stated that Adam was perfectly able but unconcerned with talking. He said that his sister talks so much that Adam just easily goes along with the flow. He asked about our daily habits and said that I supplied all his needs. He thought that Adam just didn't feel the need to talk. One day, Adam and I were upstairs. He looked up with his beautiful eyes and started singing the ABC song. The whole thing from start to finish including, "next time won't you sing with me?" He had never even attempted it before. He did not even have a couple of failed tries. YEAH! So I excitedly rushed him downstairs, plopped him in front of my mom and told her that he sang the whole ABC song. Turning to Adam, I begged him to do it again. By now he was content to play cars and was not one bit interested in my request. Nope, not one note. In fact, that little bugger did not talk for three days after that. But that was Adam.

The judge decides to talk one on one with the kids. I explain that Adam does not talk much. It is not that he cannot, it is just that he chooses not to. So the judge opens the day by calling the attorneys, the children, and the court reporter back to his chambers. We, the parents, stay in the courtroom. My children are led away from me by my attorney, but I know I can trust him. Not the attorney, yes he is a believer and totally capable of taking my children back there, but I am trusting Him. God is the only One in control here. I know that because I keep reminding myself. Over and over again I am praying every verse that He brings to my mind. *Peace Lord, please give me peace that surpasses all understanding, especially my own! Thank you for teaching me to memorize Your Word!*

Then the door opens and bouncing back to me are my brown eyed beauties with smiles on their faces, and into my arms, they land. *Thank you, Jesus!* With a quick swing of the gavel, the judge announces that the children will remain in their Christian school and be allowed to go to church. Then stating that after talking with Aalia, that she stated that she is a Christian, and shall remain as one. Her little brother didn't talk so he gets to be treated the same. BAM! Objection your honor! Here it goes I think! Then the judge just flat out states to the ex that he cannot interfere with the children and their faith. They have clearly chosen their path and that he cannot take them to the mosque, or influence them, or teach them anything else until they are eighteen. BAM! There He goes! Watching God provide where you do not think that there is any way possible for there to be a good outcome, and it hits you like a gavel! BAM! Trust Him! He is the only One you can trust, put your full faith in, and have Him show up in the courtroom, not visible to the naked eye, but glowing in full glory, and you can see Him if you have been given eyes to see and ears to hear. *Thank you, Jesus!*

      I later pay for a copy of the court transcript that was taken in the judge's chamber. It was very much God using a six-year-old vessel to say what He desired to be said. The judge asked her what religion she belongs to. "I don't belong to a religion; I have a relationship with Jesus. He lives in my heart, and when I die, I get to live with Him forever." The judge, "What does it mean to have a relationship with Jesus?" Aalia says, "It means that He is your Lord, and you follow Him, and He is your Savior because He died on the cross for your sins." "Do you know what a sin is?" "Yes, it's when you do something that you are not supposed to do. God tells you what to do, and you are supposed to obey Him, and when you don't, you sin." He asks, "Are you a sinner?" Aalia, "Yes, everyone is. For all have fallen short of the glory of God. That means everyone, you, and me, and Adam." "Do you know what it means to be a Christian?" "Yes, it means that you follow Jesus Christ. You love Him, and He loves you." "Why do you go to church Aalia?" "To learn more about God and how to study our Bible." It went on and on, question after question and brilliant answer after brilliant answer. She stood firm in her faith. She was strong and courageous and such a tiny warrior for Jesus. Even to this day I type this and tear up for God's Word is living and true. "For I know the plans I have for you." declares the Lord, "plans to prosper you and not to harm you, plans to give you a hope and a future." Jeremiah 29:11

      Looking back I can't help but be amazed at the opportunities that God created for His character to show up in a courtroom that traditionally rejects God's ways. If you want a prayer to be answered, pray directly from the Bible using Scripture. His Word is truth, and if you pray His Word, you pray Him. God can't help but bless you with Him if you are praying Him and seeking Him. What a blessing to have Him in my days. I can't imagine a day without Him!

"As for God, His ways are perfect; the Word of the LORD is flawless. He is a shield for all who take refuge in Him."

2 Samuel 22:31 (NIV)

Court - Round Two

Ok, I realize that I was trying to put years of legal battling into one chapter, but obviously, I failed. It is hard to put so much of what God did, and who He is, into just one chapter. I should have known that! But as I write there is a second marker that happened in this journey that was so huge it deserves its own chapter. Better yet, it deserves to mark my heart forever in a way that I will forever look back and "know that He is God."

Our last day in court has arrived. Today is the day that custody should be decided. I have been praying and praying hard. My brothers and sisters in Christ are praying. I have quickly realized that in my situation there is no product, no self-help book, no formula or equation that is going to make everything turn out all right. Nothing this world can offer is going to both bring my family a hope and a future and bring God glory. So I read the Bible for comfort, strength, and healing my hurts. I pray and vent to God and sit and listen to Him speak songs to my heart. I find out what grace means. Grace is unmerited favor. Grace is learning to love and to pray for your enemy, or in this case, your ex, to be treated the way you wish to be treated. Grace is love and mercy given to me by God, not because I have earned it, but because He desires me to share in the divine life with Him.

So we go into the courtroom and very quickly it takes a major turn down some really bad bunny trails. All of a sudden things that had been decided and finalized were being revisited. Wait! I am in shock that this can even come up. How can we be discussing what was not on the agenda for the day? Doesn't anyone want to follow the rules? My heart is ever aware that God has clearly shown me that I was never to "make" things happen in man's courtroom. My attorney is shocked as well. One thing after another and it just gets worse and worse.

Then all of a sudden my attorney turns to me and says that he is going to ask for a short break. We both agree and think it best to stop the man-made madness and get alone with God. Granting a recess, we have fifteen minutes to rest. I know it does not sound long, but God does not need much time to alter my future.

I go out to the hallway; my attorney goes off to the restroom. I wave everyone off wanting to be alone. I am on the second floor of a large stone building with marble floors and huge old staircases. I go over to the balcony railing. Grasping onto the railing as if I am going to give birth to a baby, I start to cry out to God. "What is happening, Lord? Why can't you stop this? Why are you not just letting this finish today? Can't you just come down and break up the madness and prove to everyone in that courtroom that you are the Most High God? Everyone thinks I am a nutcase to believe so wholeheartedly in You. Why can't you come and show them what You've shown me?" On and on I blabber.

Tears in my eyes and pain in my heart I keep crying out to Him. "He won't even say Your Name! I say Jesus now. I believe in You! I have given up so much to be with You! He wants to take my kids away from me so that they are not with You or me! I want my children to be raised up in You! He wants them to be raised in something other than You! I want them to be followers of You! He doesn't want them to have a future in You! I want them to have You in their futures!" Still sobbing my prayer turns. My heart is breaking, and I am getting desperate. I begin to beg and plead. "Lord, please let me win this. Please let me keep custody of my children. Please let them be raised up in You. Please help me God, he won't even call on You to help him, and I am begging you!"

My prayers take another turn. A mean one. "Why can't you let me win? After all, I follow You, and he doesn't. You should favor me over him! You should let me win because I am going to live with You forever and he is not. You need to choose me over him! I deserve this. I have chosen You, so You should choose me!"

And alas, one more turn. Tired, desperate, hopeless, and now angry, my prayers turn bitter. "You know what, I don't believe what You said in John 3:16 is true." "For God so loved the world that He gave His only begotten Son that whomsoever believes in Him shall not perish but have everlasting life."" Insert humph here. Half exhaustion and half frustration I let out a noise, a breath of defiance. Yes, I know what you are thinking, you just challenged the God of the Universe Himself and said that He is not what He says He is, and you used His own Word. Part of me honestly expected to get squished right there on the second floor by God's thumb. I thought God would be justified to squish me and shut me up. The other part of me honestly wished it would happen. I could not bear a life without my children, and with that thought, I open my mouth one…more…time.

"You know if You *loved me*…actually, I do not believe You love me like the Bible says. Because, if You loved me, You would let me win. You would love me more than You love him because I am a Christian and he is not. Better yet, if You loved me, You would not let him take away my children. If You loved me, You would know that my children mean the world to me, and You would not let anyone take my world away. Better yet, if You really loved me, You would not have given me children to take away from me. Ah, better yet again! If You really loved me, You would not have let me get married to the man that I would have children with, so that he would then take them away from me!" Humph again! Yes, rebellion and defiance with an ounce of pride for good measure and I stand there breathing hard and my heart racing. Alone. Or so I thought. And that is when I hear it.

"I told you don't do it."

That voice, I know that voice. Yada in Hebrew means to know and intimately understand. It is the same voice that said that there were no safety belts, and I disobeyed and got into the car anyway. It is that voice that said "Don't do it" when I was getting married, and I disobeyed and got married anyway. It is the voice that belongs to Him who created me, and I knew it! In a swift and graceful melt, I felt every bit of the glory of the moment, and I went down the railings into a pile of me on the marble floor. When God's glory shows up and shows you where you are wrong, you can't help but go down. Your knees go out, and you cannot remain standing in His presence. I know that voice!

Now in a pile of me on a cold marble floor I am sobbing. "I am so sorry Lord. I know that you love me. I am wrong. In that simple phrase, "I told you don't do it." Everything that I had gone through that was hard was my own fault, and His words revealed that to me in that moment of glory. I knew I was disobedient and that God loved me. I knew that disobedience is a sin, and I was a sinner. I knew that I could repent of my sin and be forgiven, but even a forgiven person still has to live out the consequences of their sin. Right now in this courtroom, I am living out my disobedience to the Lord who told me not to get married. And I knew it. I blamed God for "letting me get married and having children with someone who would eventually want to take them from me," and I know now that it is actually my fault.

My heart was quickened "to know" and to intimately understand that I was so wrong, that God does love the world, the whole world, and everyone He has ever created...equally showing them each individually that He created them and sent His Son Jesus to die for each of them. My flesh wanted Him to differentiate between me, the believer, and him the non-believer, but that is not in God's character. That is not who He is. He loves the whole world that means me and my ex. He loves us both equally. I now know that too. He would not choose between loving me more than him because God is God. My flesh desired more. I am the selfish one. I am the one who challenged God, and God reminded me with His voice that I was disobedient. I know that too.

So I gather myself up, wash my face, and prepare to go into the courtroom. I am prepared to face my consequences. I am prepared to lose. I am prepared to suffer. I know I am wrong, and I have just experienced a most loving and much-needed God-spanking. So I tuck my pride in my pocket, steady my nerves, and breathe. *Lord, I am so sorry, and yes, You told me don't do it. If I had obeyed You, then I would not be here in this place, and You would not have to show up on the balcony to remind me that You really are who You are and that I need never to forget that You are love.*

Court starts back, but I am lost in my thoughts. God has a way of changing me when He touches me. My heart is broken and healed at the same time. I challenged the very Word of God. I now look in love over to the other side of the room and wonder for the first time how he is feeling right now. I have just been changed forever and heard from The Judge, another one of God's names. It seems unimportant to sit here and listen to this judge, but I do.

The courtroom judge holds up a stack of papers so thick that his hands are struggling. He declares that the northern state must have had a reason for granting the mother full custody, so he has decided to uphold their decision. The mother shall retain full legal and custodial custody and that the father shall get unsupervised visitation. Details to be worked out with my ruling. BAM! The gavel crashes, and he up and leaves the room. I sit there in awe. Not in him, but of Him!

It is over. Years of fighting and it is finished. The attorney's talk, the papers are filed, the court reporter types away, and we gather up to leave the room. Going out of the room I look over to that spot on the balcony. I cried out there. I challenged the very essence of who God is there. I got told, so to speak, there. I melted there. I realized my sinful nature there. I repented there. I saw God's plan there. His plan includes salvation for all of us. Salvation through Jesus comes for my children and me, for my ex and the attorneys, for the judge and the court reporter and everyone else in that room who will listen to His voice.

"Here I Am! I stand at the door and knock. If anyone hears My voice and opens the door, I will come in and eat with him, and he with Me."

Revelation 3:20 (NIV)

Looking back, I can't help but be in awe of God. He placed something in my past; the "Don't do it," so that in my future when I reached a major turning point in my journey with Him I could "remember what He has done." God knew and intimately understood that I would reach a fork in my faith journey, a crossroads in which I could turn bitter and angry at God and go down the path of being saved but useless because I had not learned what love is and that He is love.

Or I could know and intimately understand that God has been very much with me along this journey, and it really was my own fault when I stepped out in disobedience, and I did not listen to His voice. If on that day on that balcony you would have told me that my life would forever be changed by a "recess" when I heard the same voice from my past tell me in my present what was His plan and that it would affect my future, I would have said, "No way. You can't change a life forever in fifteen minutes." However, God is not defined by time because He created time. He is up to something good, and it includes us all!

Sometimes there are events in our lives that have the potential to squeeze every bit of hope and belief in God out of us. But God's plan is that we do not get to that place and stand there alone. We stand at that place with belief almost disappearing, and if we still have hope in Him, we will make it out of that darkness to walk in His Light. Well, God showed up, and there is no way to explain it except that He is good.

Driving home, my poor mother was so upset about my loss of supervised visitation! I reminded her that God was in control, and I had not lost that which was truly important. What is important is having a say in how the children would be raised and that they would be raised in Him. My mother then started to tell me that she does not know how I handle all that keeps coming my way. How can I have such peace in such trying circumstances? And ends with I don't know how you do it but I want that! *THAT! I know how you can get "that!" His Name is Jesus, I declare, and we pull off the highway to pray together! BAM! God is just showing off now!*

"Whoever does not love does not know God, because God is love. This is how God showed His love among us: He sent His one and only Son into the world that we might live through Him. This is love: not that we loved God, but that He loved us and sent His Son as an atoning sacrifice for our sins. Dear friends, since God so loved us we also ought to love one another. No one has ever seen God; but if we love one another, God lives in us and His love is made complete in us."

1 John 4:8-12 (NIV)

"We know that we live in Him and He is us, because He has given us of His Spirit. And we have seen and testify that the Father has sent His Son to be the Savior of the world. If anyone acknowledges that Jesus is the Son of God, God lives in him and he in God. And so we know and rely on the love God has for us."

1 John 4:13-16 (NIV)

"God is love. Whoever lives in love lives in God, and God in him. In this way, love is made complete among us so that we will have confidence on the day of judgment, because in this world we are like Him. There is no fear in love. But perfect love drives out fear, because fear has to do with punishment. The one who fears is not made perfect in love."

1 John 4:16-18 (NIV)

"We love because He first loved us. If anyone says, "I love God," yet hates his brother, he is a liar. For anyone who does not love his brother, whom he has seen, cannot love God, who he has not seen. And He has given us this command: Whoever loves God must also love his brother."

1 John 4:19-21 (NIV)

Single Parent Conference

The kids are going on their first unsupervised visitation with their father. I pack their new bags. Small rolling suitcases, Adam's is blue and red, and Aalia's is pink and purple. Both sets of bags include the necessities like fresh clothes, pajamas, and toiletries. They each pick out their "sleeping buddy" for the weekend. Aalia picks out a kitten and Adam picks out "Will," the pig. Now, before I go on, let me explain Will, the pig. We acquired this pink beanie baby pig from a neighbor as a gift to Aalia for her birthday. Aalia did not pay much attention to it. She had other favorites. But when Adam was very small, he crawled over to her stash of critters and picked out a pink beanie pig from her pile, and fought for dear life to keep it. Aalia did not want it, but she did not want Adam to have it either. Siblings are so much fun to have. Eventually, she forgot to care about Adam and his new pig. Adam dragged that pink pig everywhere. Will the pig became his go-to nighttime buddy. It was just natural to send it with him. He always slept with it. Will the pig has been with us for years now.

Now back to where we are in the story. I have packed their bags. I have steadied myself to be able to let go of my babies for the weekend. It will be a long weekend for me, but I trust the Lord, and He is in control. Lots of tears and the children are buckled up. They are ready for a new adventure. That first night is so hard. The house is so quiet. I have time to myself. No bathing brown babies. No bedtime stories. None of the normal bedtime routines. Then the phone rings. It is late, and I wonder who it is. It is the ex. He is very upset that I have packed a pink pig in his son's suitcase. Don't forget my baggage, people! How dare I do such a disgraceful thing? Obviously, I was intentionally evil and planned the abomination. So we argue, he threatens to throw the pig away, and I try to explain calmly how Adam has acquired said evil beanie abomination. I can hear him crying in the background. "Kids just pick their own favorite nighttime buddies," I try to explain in vain. Explanations lead to pleading not to wreck the beanie, and I will drive the 45-mile trip to retrieve the beanie pig if he will NOT throw it away. I also try to explain that Adam will not sleep without it. I remind him that I need to get dressed and get gas in the car and that it will take me some time to get there but that I will be coming right away. We hang up.

I start to pray, and I begin to worry about Adam crying. Nothing breaks a mother's heart like her child's tears, and I feel very helpless. I can see those beautiful brown eyes with the long eyelashes filling up with tears that hang at the corners as his bottom lip comes up in a pout. A few minutes pass. I get dressed and get my purse, and as I go out the door, I hear the phone ring. It's their dad; he says don't bother coming. Adam has stopped crying, and he is asleep now. I pause and then ask where the pig is. "In the bed with Adam," and he hangs up. The kids return on Sunday along with Will, the pig. We have just begun a new season in which every other weekend Aalia, Adam, and Will the pig visit their Muslim dad.

As time goes on, I am learning to "be a good Christian." I write that in jest because I look back and think what a dork I was. I was acting like the vast majority of the Christians that I was exposed to. You know the ones, they have comfort zones and book clubs, vacation together and eat out together and call it fellowship. Why can't I be strong and stand in what God Himself shows me, like power and glory in the courtroom, or on the side of the highway? But I do not, and I cave. Which in my world, I think, means that I have to do what the others are doing. So I buy a t-shirt, get the fish on the back of my truck, and I listen to Christian music and read Christian books. I even decide to attend a Christian conference put on by Focus on the Family for Single Parents. I have never been to a Christian conference before.

The weeks leading up to the conference were stressful. I had just survived by the grace of God, literally, "the courtroom." I was busy working, and I had taken on some part-time jobs when the kids were visiting their dad. I would landscape and garden for others. I would paint rooms with Bible verses on walls. I would bake cakes and babysit. Anything to make some extra money. Did I mention that I worked for a church? So I work. I work hard and long, and I get very tired. Pretty soon I learn a new term, "burn out." Ugh, I have by-passed comfort zone, but walk head first directly into burn out." I am too tired to study my Bible and my prayer time usually lands me in a nap. Something has got to change, and since God never changes, it must be me.

My friend tells me about this conference. They are going to tell single parents about spiritual warfare, prayer, budgeting, and all kinds of other things. I am so tired that the night before I decide that I am too tired to attend. As I read my Bible, I realize that the very thing that my tired body needs is to rest and learn more about Him. So I fall asleep determined to attend.

Wake up call. I wake up and get ready to go. I pray about what God has planned for me, and the word "determination" comes to mind. The kids are away for the weekend, and I am traveling about an hour away to a church that I have never been to before. As I am driving, the radio is playing Christian song after Christian song and ministering to my heart. I feel as if someone knew my inner thoughts and put them to music. I have cried tears of joy and pain, relief and anger all the while driving to this unknown place. It takes much effort to get there. I have since learned that when God wishes to "move" you to a new place, it often takes great effort.

My car is old and begins to act up. It has not had anything wrong with it but seems to lose power whenever I have to slow down. When I stop at a stop light or stop sign so does my car. I have left early enough, so I am not worried about time, just the car. This is before cell phones. As I get within twenty or so miles of the church, I enter a town. This means lots of people, lots of cars, and lots of stops. Again, every time I am coming to a stop I try not to. I just drive slowly up and hope the light turns or stop at the sign and my car dies. Each time I am praying for it to restart. I know nothing about cars.

So, the dance begins. I drive, I pray, I have to slow down, I pray harder. I stop. The car stops. I pray and beg God and the car starts. Repeat the cycle. Pretty soon I am rebuking the devil. Time is sliding away, and it is close to the start time and the time it takes to revive the car gets longer and longer. I pray in the Name of Jesus that my car starts, and it does. I rebuke the enemy and tell him that I don't care what he has planned for me today, God's plans are bigger and better. The cycle continues to repeat, with the church in sight, I start singing God's praises. The last words out of my mouth go something like this: "Let everything that has breath (and gas) praise the Lord. Praise the Lord!" My car is dead, and I coast into the parking spot in silence. I don't care if it is dead. God told me, "determination." I remind the devil of that several times. I had to remind myself many more times than that. "I will deal with you later I thought," and rush into the church which is a tent. Just in time to start.

The conference is better than I could have ever imagined. I get real advice for budgeting. Most advice on budgeting your money to single parents goes something like this. Cut back on your entertainment expenses, cut back on eating out, and on your wardrobe. Don't use your department store credit cards, and pay cash for your large purchases, etc. All of which is good, if you actually had an entertainment budget, etc. Mine is PBS and videos from the church library. Eating out, that's good too if that counts paper bagging it to work and the amount you put in your bag. Your kids come first, and restaurants are what daddy takes you to because mommy can't afford it.

The wardrobe one is funny. Thank God that I am working for a church. I dressed in church t-shirts handed out at every camp, or event, or even the events that had leftovers that they did not know what to do with. They make great PJ's for me and the kids depending on sizes. The bigger, the better. Some we wore for years and years, and you can tell which ones those were because in pictures of the kids you would see ankles, then knees, then thighs, then shorts would stretch the shirt one more year. Genius! And the kid's wardrobe was school uniforms. Simple and easy. A few church outfits and two or three shoes each. We did not do fancy anything. But God provided. He is faithful that way!

The next two are easy, do not do any credit cards and do not make any large purchases. That makes it simple. But today is different. Stressing the importance that my money is actually God's money and that His provision is something that I need to be aware of, thankful for, and careful with. Giving back to the Lord is very important. It shows that you trust Him completely, and He does not care how much because it is all already His.

I also learn that praying to God about what I financially need is good, but praying about how I spend what I already have is better. I once prayed that I would have enough in my checking account that I did not have to watch every penny. I am not talking hundreds of thousands, or even millions or billions. I was talking about a few extra hundred or even a thousand. I thought it would be such a relief and very grand to feel like I did not have to worry about what was in there. After my prayer I was quiet, and the Holy Spirit spoke to me. "If I had enough in my bank account that I did not have to think about it, then would I still talk to God about every penny in that account?" "Probably not," I honestly answer. That is the point; I do not want to think about it! "Then if you didn't think about it, you wouldn't pray about it, and you wouldn't talk to ME about it would you?" Nope. Then the Holy Spirit said, "But when you talk to me about it, and I help you, we are communicating, and that is what makes a relationship. In money terms, we are investing in one another." Wow!

Another part of the conference talked about dating. Ugh, let's not go there now. But they did not listen to me, and they did. Again such a different attitude toward what I had read on single parenting and dating. I never really dated and I am as awkward as all get out and so not good in new or nervous situations. The whole idea of dating makes my head spin. Then the speaker speaks of first loving the Lord with all your heart, soul, mind, and strength. Then loving yourself, and then only if the Lord has shown you that you have the other two areas handled, should you move forward with dating. Yeah! I am so happy and content to just keep falling more and more in love with my Savior, and the stress it takes off of me is huge. Now the loving myself part is harder to handle. I still feel the sting of "shame" that I have inherited, and that is going to take more time.

Then a most amazing thing happens. There are about two hundred of us ladies of all ages in this tent. Obviously, we are all mothers, but some of us are new moms, and some of us have been moms for a while. The speaker is announced. Thelma Wells is her name. Now I try not to put too many names in this book because I hope that you will walk away from reading this book and remember only The One Who Is The Name Above All Names. This book is about what God has done. But Thelma Wells does a most loving and wonderful thing which deserves to be repeated. She is the second half of the day right after lunch. She speaks for around ten minutes, and while she speaks you could hear some noises in the back of the tent, we are in.

It starts small, a few coos, and then some little noises get louder and louder. Every mother in the room knows the sound. It is the frustration noise that a newborn makes before they burst forth in tears and crying and fill the tent with the sound of a baby. I am sure that some are thinking, "Why didn't she get a babysitter like everyone else?" Still, others are thinking, "Why didn't the conference offer daycare?" I am thinking, actually praying, that the baby will not make the speaker mad. I have seen that before. Our pastor will always stop and announce that we have a really good preschool ministry. Probably not the most loving response, but I am expecting the same from Thelma. The baby gets louder, and every mother in the room gets nervous for the mother.

Thelma Wells stops speaking mid-sentence just as the baby gets very, very loud. *Oh God, please help her*, as the whole room, including the speaker, turns her direction. My heart breaks for her as I see how incredibly young she is, more than likely the youngest woman in the room. *Please, God, don't let Thelma be mad, I pray!* Then she does it, that most wonderful thing that still brings my very much older self to tears as I type these words and remember this day. She does turn toward the crying baby, but instead of being ugly she glows like Jesus. Thelma Wells says, "Young lady... (Everyone in the room is holding their breath) Has anyone ever told you, thank you for choosing life!" And she continues to speak as if the baby is a most welcomed member under the covering. I can't even type clearly right now through my salty tears. *Thank you, Jesus, for spell check and Thelma. Thank you, Jesus, for that young girl and her little baby.* Thelma Wells may have directed that comment to the young girl, but there are many more ears and hearts in that room that need to hear that comment. This includes me. Every time I am tired, or even doubt, I remember the crying of the little ones and remember, Jesus would say that too, "Thank you, Shahe, for choosing life!"

Looking back, God needed to speak to me in a new way. It was not the typical pie chart or bullet point lesson, but how to handle flaming arrows from the enemy himself. He showed me how to love one another as you wish to be loved yourself. I walked away filled with renewed hope, encouragement, and with the idea that we were a complete family even when society labels us as incomplete, if you have Jesus, and He is your bridegroom, then you are married to Him. He is your other parent for your children and from that day forward I expected that of Him. And He says in His Word that He will supply all my needs and never leave me nor forsake me. I consider that to be a great relationship. I call that a pretty good marriage.

And just in case you were wondering about my car, well I never gave it a second thought the whole day. As I walked out full of His Word, I suddenly remembered and thought, "What am I going to do about this car? How will I get home?" So I got in, turned it on and drove it all the way home with not one bit of trouble. It did not stop once. It did not even putter or make a funny noise. So I rolled down my windows and sang loudly and praised Jesus all the way home. Nothing, I tell you, is impossible with my God!

"Let your conduct be without covetousness; be content with such things as you have. For He Himself has said, "I will never leave you nor forsake you."

Hebrews 13:5 (NKJV)

Dancing With My Father And For My Father

Time moves on. It is 1998. The children and I love our church home. They love their school. We are settling into a routine of visitations every other weekend with their dad. This leaves me with some time on my hands. I am working at the church for Mr. Richard, and the planning for the Passion Play begins. I find out that they need people to dance in the play, so I join the group. I love to dance. We rehearse for months leading up to Resurrection Sunday (I will not call it Easter, that is a pagan name, and there is nothing pagan about my Jesus. But an explanation will have to wait for later, maybe next to the Santa chapter). I become one of the Jewish dancing girls that dances and sings during the songs that bridge between sections of the storyline of the Passion Play. Me, a Jewish dancing girl in a Christian play!

The more we practice, the more we dance, the more I read my Bible, the more I realize how important God's plan was during the Passover season that becomes the crucifixion and ultimately Resurrection Sunday. I am studying God's Word in a new way. I am learning about my Jesus who is Jewish. Was Jesus a Jew? Who knew?

As the play approaches, I begin asking the Lord for my father to hear the Gospel. I put his name on the prayer list for the play participants which include the choir, orchestra, and church staff. One of the days before the play I am working in the resource room with a co-worker who asks about my dad and is he coming to see the play? I am using the die cutter and making lots, and lots of die cuts out of colored construction paper. I answer that I have invited him, but my prayer is that he stays through the intermission, I just want him to hear the story of Jesus. I am afraid that the intermission break is long, and that he will sneak out. My co-worker reminds me that "Nothing is impossible with God." And as I cut the next die cut, I realize that I am putting God in a box. How did I realize that? Because I am limiting Him and what He can do as I am cutting out box after box on the die-cut machine.

Saturday night comes around, the choir, orchestra, dancers, animal handlers, staff, counselors, stage crew, etc. gather together to pray. The choir pastor asks if my dad is here and I say yes, I saw him in the front row center. So we pray for him by name and the play begins. The whole play I am consumed with "don't let him leave at intermission Lord," as I dance and sing and hit all my marks. I even take a hit on my bare right foot from Jesus himself, well the actor Jesus, who has sandals on and his buckle left me bleeding. But I dance on. Intermission comes and goes, and he comes back. I can see him as I dance. Every time I pass someone, they whisper, "I'm praying for your dad." Even as the play progresses, and on stage the whispers continue, my heart is full, and it is about to be overflowing as the big finale is coming.

The Passion Play has a moment in it after the cross where the High Priest stops the play and starts the narrative about God's plan for salvation. This allows all of the actors and dancers to go quickly off stage and change into their eternity whites. The dancers become the heavenly angels. I get to have a high spot on the mountain, and I have very long clothes with tons of white fabric. I have big wings with dowels in them to make my wings even larger. I am a walking ball of white fabric. While the High Priest is on stage laying out the plan of salvation, he slowly removes his high priest clothing and puts on his modern-day watch, jacket, and shoes. This particular night it is one of my most favorite pastors. I've introduced you all before. He is my favorite, big, tall, white guy.

I position myself in my assigned spot. I am the first angel to go through the heavy stage curtains as the Pastor/High Priest asks the audience to bow their heads, and he prays. He is not quite there yet, but I am ready to go up my mountain and get into position while the audience is praying (I have learned that's what Christian's do!). The stagehand happens to be Mary, eldest daughter of pastor big tall, white guy. She asks, "Are you excited?" "Yes," I reply. She asks, "Do you want to pray?" Pray? She gets down on her knees, and I just stare at her. My mind is racing, but I am thinking, "If I go down on my knees in this mass of white and wings, I might not be able to get back up, and forget about clean. This floor has had goats and camels and critters all over it." But she starts to pray, and I go down. I hit my knees. Eyes closed, I release the white and wings and just go to His throne. She is praying so sweetly for my father's salvation, and I remember thinking, "Nothing is impossible with God." I then feel the most wonderful, cool, sweet breeze brush my face. It feels like a kiss and love and glory all in a quick breath. I open my eyes thinking that the breeze is impossible because of the heavy unopened stage curtains. Where did that breeze come from?

There is my cue, heads are bowed, someone opens the curtain, and I in my white and my wings climb the mountain. I am on the right side of the cross as you look at the stage, and my wings are forward and covering my face, yet, because they are sheer, I can see my father. I thank the Lord for him and that he stayed through intermission. I pray that the Lord touch his heart so that he can be saved too. There is just something wonderful about the final heaven scene. Jesus rides in on his white horse, we dance, and sing His praises, the audience is on their feet clapping, and I get a tiny taste of what heaven must be like. Believers in unity, worshiping the King of Kings. I think, "It doesn't get any better than this." But God thinks differently than I do and He has a much better plan.

At the end of the play, we go out and greet the audience, shake hands, and take pictures. This is my first play, so this is new to me. I quickly find my dad, and we are standing there talking. He likes my wings and says that he needs to talk to me. About what I ask? Well he says, I prayed that prayer....wait "what prayer," I ask? Just then Jill comes up and asks if she can take a picture of my dad and me together and I say sure. She takes a couple of shots (film camera days), and the whole time I am thinking what prayer! She leaves, and I ask. Dad, what prayer? The prayer the big, tall, white guy prayed. Yes, I am my father's daughter.

Seriously? Well, give me a chance to change and we can talk! He tells me to meet him across the street at the Cracker Barrel, and I rush back to the dressing room half in tears and totally unable to get my stuff in order for tomorrow. I decide to pile it in a corner, and I will deal with it early tomorrow, after all, I work here. I'll just come in early. So off to Cracker Barrel I rush. I pull in, and we get seated quickly. We order and I am major league questioning him. Dad, which prayer? Which big, tall, white guy? Which God? When? Are you sure? Do you know what this means? Do you know what you have done? A million questions from the queen of questions.

He answers them all. He is choosing Jesus, and I am in total shock. I just cannot get over that he has actually chosen Jesus! This can't be real! I hope it's real, but this can't be real! Our waitress comes toward us with our food on a tray. I remember glancing over there and seeing a whole fish. Now, I don't even remember what my father ordered, but I distinctly remember seeing a whole fish just as I was thinking, "can my dad really choose Jesus in one night?" I see the waitress lose control of the tray and everything crashes down right in front of our table.

Now the old me comes back, the ten-year-old me that used to hide under the table when my Muslim father gave service workers a hard time for not doing something right. My brother and I used to cringe whenever that side of him came out, and right now I am dying inside for this waitress. I am sure he is about to let her have it. But that is when his change becomes evident. My dad, the one who would have yelled and belittled her, bent down and helped her pick it up. She is proclaiming how sorry she is, and he is helping her pick up the mess saying it is ok. Is this my dad? Can my dad change? Just as I think that, he looks up from the floor; just his head appears above the table, and his face glows. His worry lines on his forehead are gone. I do not remember him without those lines, but his face is smooth, and he glows. He smiles, and he is at peace, and I can tell he has been made new. He tells the waitress just to bring him some soup, and we continue to talk.

We finish eating and hug goodbye. I cannot stop squealing in excitement for what He has done. I think he, my dad, is surprised to see how excited I am. He does not know what I do. He is about to have his life turned upside down in a most magnificent way, and I cannot contain myself. I drive home just praising the Lord for all He has done for my father, for me, for my family. Then as I am driving the flesh creeps in. I am doing my normal talk/prayer, 90 mph speed talking/praying to God. *"God this is so cool. You are so good. I can't believe this is real. Is this real God? I don't want to go to church tomorrow and tell people that my father has chosen You if this is not real. I don't want to lie to people that trust me if this is not real! I can't believe this Lord. Can my dad really be saved in one night?"* 90 mph and pushing 100 mph. I rattle on and on. Then I come to a stop light, but just before I come to a complete stop, a car comes out of a parking lot and pulls right in front of me and stops at the light. We are the only two cars on the road at about 1 a.m. I am blabbing to God and asking if this is real and this real car gets right in front of me. Ugh, I think. Couldn't he have waited? So I quickly brake to a stop, and we sit there. All the while I am still asking God if this is real when I realize we have sat at this red light forever. Ugh, this is the longest red light ever. But then I take notice of the car ahead of me. We sit, we wait, and then I look down at the license plate. It says "GODSREL." Wait…what?

The very second I see the license plate "GODSREL" the light turns green, and he pulls into the intersection and makes a right turn. What? That didn't make sense! He pulled off to the right which was the direction he came from. He had no actual reason to pull out in front of me because the parking lot he pulled out from has another entrance which would have taken him down that very street. But God had other plans. I needed God's confirmation.

Looking back God intended for me to have that car pull out in front of me so that I would see the answer to my question, "Is this real God?" And yes, "GOD IS REAL!" Wow! I no longer questioned my father's salvation. I had two confirmed markers showing that he had truly been saved tonight. Who am I to keep God in a box and pray for my father to stay through intermission? What a limiting prayer! My God, who by the way is real, is limitless and nothing, and I mean nothing, is impossible for Him! I returned Sunday morning and put up an "It's a boy!" poster on the staff information board. This is what it said:

It's A Boy!

It is with much prayer, praise, and thanksgiving to Almighty God that I, Shahe, proudly announce the spiritual birth of my father Mohammad on April 4, 1998. He prayed the Sinner's Prayer during the evening performance of the Passion Play. He was a Muslim for 57 years. I want to thank with all of my heart this wonderful church, the people that have been praying for him, the choir for praying for him before the performance, everyone involved in the play that touched my father's heart, and most of all my Lord and Savior Jesus Christ for giving me another miracle! I love you with all of my heart! Nothing is impossible with God. Luke 1:37.

You could not make my feet touch the ground for the next week. I floated everywhere! On Wednesday night during service, I walked behind the "Redeemer" banner and gave a brief testimony of my father's salvation. He came back the following Saturday to see the play again, but before it started, he wanted to tell everyone, thank you. I brought him back to the choir room where we all gathered to pray before the performance started. They handed him a microphone, and my father proclaimed Jesus as his Lord and Savior to everyone in that room. It was wonderful. He was baptized the very next day by my favorite big, tall white guy. How great was that! I have proof too, pictures of my father being baptized! Wow, God is so good. And real by the way, just in case you still have any doubts. And if you do, you just need to get over it (yourself) because it is true.

The Sunday of my father's baptism is also the last performance of the Passion Play for that year. I am so sad it is ending, I never want it to end. What a blessing this week has been. I get to pray and see my prayers answered over and over again. Each time exceedingly and abundantly in ways that my mind could never have come up with on my own. But my heart is full, my feet are floating, and I put away the Jewish Dancing girl in a Christian church, and started my drive home. As I am driving, I am praying. I am talking to God, and yes, at 90 mph (the praying part not the driving part). I start by thanking God for all that He has done. I thank Him for my parents' salvation and my children's salvation. I thank Him for the Redeemer banner and for the fish that fell from the tray. I thank Him for godly influences that share the Good News of the Gospel of Jesus Christ to those that need to hear. I thank Him for everything from the car I am driving to the new scar on my foot.

I come up to the stop light where I saw the license plate a week ago. *"Do you remember this place, Lord? This is where that car pulled out, and I sat there forever at the red light until I finally looked down and saw the plate say "GODSREL" just as I was asking you if my dad was really saved and is this really real, God? Do you remember God?"* Now, I know full well God remembers, but sometimes I am just, well me. As I pull closer, the light changes from green to yellow, to red. "Oh yeah, this is also the world's longest red light," I joke just as another car pulls out of that same parking lot right in front of me again. Just me and a car and the red light. Well, actually, it is me, the other car, the red light, and GOD!

"Yup, just waiting, how cool are You, God! Remember this; we sat here forever until I finally looked down at the license plate and…" And then it happens again. I look down, and there it is. The license plate reads, "CUNHVEN." Now it is just me, and a car, and the red light, and God, and tears, tears, tears. I just sit here and cry as the red light turns green, the car again turns right, and I thank God that someday we will see one another again in heaven. God is so good!

Looking back I can't help but type with excitement. God exceeded every expectation and prayer that was prayed. He always does if you let Him. My earthly father now belongs to my Heavenly Father, and it doesn't get any better than that. Jill gave me the pictures once she got her roll of film developed. It was months later, and in all of the excitement, we both forgot about them. But to my surprise was the banner which was behind my father and me that night when we took the picture. You see, I don't remember posing in front of a banner, but I guess we did. It was the banner I used to say was so graphic with the blood on it. It was red and gold and silver. It said "Redeemer," and it had a cross and the pierced hands of Jesus on it. It was the banner that I walked behind the night I shared at church that my father was saved. It was the banner that said it best; my father has a Redeemer, and His Name is Jesus.

Looking back Jesus did leave a mark on me, in fact, the actor Jesus left a scar on my right foot. But scars are ok. They remind you that you are healed, and you can heal. Yes, I talk to God, and that's ok too. Talking reminds you that you are in a conversation, and you can listen. Yes, I pray to God, and that is ok too. Praying reminds you that you are in a relationship with the Most High God. A believer who has a relationship with the Most High God is the ONLY follower of a faith-religion that can hear from and be in a relationship with the Living God Who created the Universe. Unless you have a real relationship with the real God, you will never get love confirmations like GODSREL and CUNHVEN. That was God's way to give me touchable confirmations that I needed to be set free in Him, both now and in our future. He did it again. He put things in my past and present so that when my future comes, I can rely on Him. I can dance with Him too!

For your Maker is your husband-the LORD Almighty is His name-the Holy One of Israel is your Redeemer, He is called the God of all the earth."

Isaiah 54:5 (NIV)

Adam Makes A Choice

I like reading testimonies of people who have encountered the Lord Jesus Christ. I love how individually the Lord can ministers to each of us. I may get a license plate or two, and you might get a song or a card. Each of us has our own "thing," or intimate touch, that is just between the Lord and us. He is just that able! One of the first books I read early in my journey was about personal testimonies of people that encountered Jesus in miraculous ways. I had also read an article about Billy Graham and how he was saved by attending revivals led by evangelist Mordecai Ham. Mordecai Ham got saved when he attended Billy Sunday's event and Billy Sunday got saved by attending a service by J. Wilbur Chapman. J. Wilbur Chapman was saved at a Dwight L. Moody event, and Dwight L Moody was saved at an Edward Kimball event. I am not sure if this is actually true, but it gets me thinking and praying. I would love for my son to preach the Gospel and share it with everyone he knows and comes in contact with. How cool would that be? What a legacy!

Did I know any of these folks and their history? No. I only recognize Billy Graham's name. He was the preacher that when he came on television, my parents would grumble and switch channels. Later, I grew up, and I flipped channels and grumbled too. I knew he preached about Jesus, but I had never listened to him, not until after I was saved. One evening he was on television, and I just sat there and cried. What sweetness I had missed! All because I quickly dismissed his gift and changed the channel. But that was a learned reaction. How many other things do we dismiss because of our way of growing up or our traditions? Let me tell you one about my great grandmother.

My "Ma" was my maternal great-grandmother. She has quite a testimony too. But for now, I will share with you a story about pie, because every time you went to her house, she would share a pie with you. Her pies were wonderful. Always homemade with love and we always looked forward to going to her home.

Because they were in the south and we lived in the north, we did not go over there as often as we would have liked. But I grew up knowing that Ma made great pies, it was one of her gifts. Each time we would go over there I would be offered Chess Pie. I did not know what that was. I was young, and honestly, I thought it was related to the board game or something. But because I did not know or understand or recognize that pie, I did not eat it. In fact, over and over and over again, I passed up her chess pie for other options. I even once asked what it was and did not get a satisfactory answer, so I never did eat that pie. I grew up, and Ma grew older, and one day I was over there, and her age was beginning to show. When I was young, there would be three or four different kinds of pie to choose from, but today there was just the Chess pie. So she smiled and offered it, and I accepted thinking I was about to die.

Well to my surprise that chess pie was not only good, but it was also delicious. It melted in my mouth and tasted like heaven. What sweetness I had missed! All those years of passing up what quickly became my most favorite thing she made. I almost missed it, a treasure that my great grandmother made with her sweet, hardworking hands all because I did not know or understand what was going on. I had quickly dismissed that pie for other options when all along that was the best choice of pie ever offered.

Don't you think God knows that? How many times does He send a believer to talk with and share with a non-believer only for that non-believer to dismiss the believer for a "better" worldly option? How many times do we change the channel to ignore His Word? How many times do we pass up the Bible on the table or pass on the opportunity to be prayed for or prayed with? How many times do we pass up that sweet opportunity that God presents which is really the best choice for us? I have done it a million times. I dismissed my American family's faith. I dismissed my Jesus' freak friends. I dismissed Billy Graham numerous times on the television. I even dismissed the Lord's own voice, and I got in that car, and I got married. I am a dis-misser. But I do not want to miss out anymore!

So, when I am awake, I am very aware of how I spend my day, how I spend my time, my resources, my energy, and where my heart is. I don't want to miss anything! So this particular day I am driving one of the church vans full of children to a rehearsal for the Billy Graham Crusade that is coming to town. Our kids along with several other churches are singing on the kid's event day, and I am helping our choir director with the driving and with the kids. I follow her van to a church I have never been to before, and we get the kids all settled in. Rehearsal begins, and of course the obvious happens. Someone has to go to the restroom. Since I'm at the end of the row of kids, I take her. She is a first grader, and we are in a strange place, so I am in my protective mode. We go off to find the restroom, and it is a large one, so I make sure no one is inside, and then I stand outside the door on guard. While waiting, I look up at the very different light fixture, and I get an overwhelming feeling of, "You are going to work here someday." What? But she is back, and we head back to the sanctuary, and I quickly dismiss the promise.

A couple of weeks later it is the big day. My babysitter for Adam, who is too young to participate, has canceled. I show up with Adam, and there is my choir director with her daughter Nicole. Nicole is the same age as Adam, and her babysitter has canceled too. So Denise smiles and puts them both in the mandatory t-shirts to blend in and because they are our kids both of them already know all of the words to all of the songs. Maybe they will just blend in she smiles. Whew, disaster averted. We load up the vans and head to the stadium.

We sing and hear the Word of God presented to everyone and every child in that stadium. How wonderful it is to have a stadium filled up with children and adults all singing to the Lord. We pray that each person there will not leave without surrendering their lives to the Lord Jesus Christ! Amen and Amen! I love the body of Jesus Christ. I can't wait for eternity when we get to worship Him all the day long! When the time for the invitation comes, we are all praying and hoping that our children will have soften hearts that are responsive to God's Word and …there he goes. Adam is going down the aisle and heading toward the stadium grass. His mind is made up; he has decided to follow

Jesus. No channel switching here! There goes my little six year old with his curly black hair, beautiful brown skin, and gorgeous white smile from ear to ear. All joy! That's my boy! That's my little overcomer! Wait….what do I do! I have dozens of kids to look after, and there goes my baby!

I look to Denise in panic and yell down the row, "What do I do?" and she smiles and grins back, "GO!" So off I go again. Chasing after the child of my womb, who just like his sister, knows beyond a shadow of a doubt to whom he belongs. He belongs to Jesus. The boldness of these children! Where did they get that from? It is not from their chicken mother who avoids aisles and decisions! They must get it from their daddy. Their Heavenly Daddy! Father God is just that good! I join Adam in the soft green grass just as a young lady sits down with him to talk to him and make sure that he understands what he is doing. We talk, listen to Adam answer her questions and he has done it. The boy who rarely talked early in his life is rambling on and on about how much he wants Jesus in his life today! We pray and I cry. They give him a Bible and some information and ask if they can follow up with him in a couple of days. Wow. My baby boy is not such a baby, but now he is a child of the Most High God! My baby boy is now my brother in Christ Jesus! Hallelujah!

Looking back I can't help but smile, rejoice, laugh and cry. My son has a hope and future. My son has an inheritance. He is the Child of the Most High God, and I get to live out eternity and share it with both Aalia and Adam. I remember that day on the balcony just outside the courtroom where I told God that I did not believe He really loved me because He allowed me to have these children just to take them away from me. In repentance, I cry as I remember today when on the floor of a sports stadium I tell God that I believe in Him and that He really loves me because He has allowed me to have these children and we get to live out eternity together. God is so good.

As I sit back down with the church kids and the chaperones, I look around. My heart is full. My arms hold a beautiful baby boy who is so excited about what he has just done, and I look around, and God reminds me of another answered prayer that I did not *even remember that I prayed, but God heard, and He remembered. I prayed that I would love for my son to preach the Gospel and share it with everyone he knows and comes in contact with. I prayed that he would have a legacy! He prayed to receive Christ at a Billy Graham crusade. And I know what you are thinking, what if he is in the line or the legacy like all those other names of people who preach the Gospel and someone gets saved, and the list of names goes on and on. But I know what I am thinking. As long as his future is in Christ Jesus, he has the greatest inheritance provided to God's creations by Him the Creator God, a gift to us all, dismissed by most, and celebrated by few. He has a hope, and a future, and His Name is Jesus!*

Please don't close this book and dismiss Him. Please taste His sweet gift of salvation! As I type these closing words, I think about so many more stories that I wish to tell you. God continues to amaze and show off and bring glory to Himself, and I would love to share these stories with you. Stories of my trips to Israel, stories of my mission trip to a closed country and how God got the Bibles in and us back out. I want to tell you how He has provided and healed, and, as I type, I realize I have been so blessed because I have so much more to share with you, enough to fill another book.

But I also realize that in a small way that is just the very thing God is trying to tell each of us. It starts with a story, a gift of a baby whose very name, Jesus, means salvation. A perfect life lived so that He could die and provide a way for us, the unholy, to live out eternity with a very Holy God. The gift is just the first page in the book. God has so many more stories that He wishes to tell you. God continues to amaze and show off and bring Himself glory after His Son has been crucified and resurrected, and He would love to share those stories with you. Stories of His trips to Damascus, stories of His mission trips to closed countries and how God gets His Holy Bible into our lives and into closed hearts. He wants to tell you how He has provided and healed, and, as I type, I realize that He has been such a blessing because He has so much more to share with you, enough to fill a book called the Bible. It is called the Holy Bible, just like its Holy Author.

I love you so very much my Jesus. Thank you, Jesus, for making me an overcomer. I pray that you too will overcome whatever you have between you and Him which is keeping you apart so that you too can know and intimately understand what an eternal joy it is to be called a child of the Most High God.

"How great is the love the Father has lavished on us, that we should be called children of God! And that is what we are! The reason the world does not know us is that it did not know Him."

1 John 3:1 (NIV)

"Yet to all who receive Him, to those who believed in His name, He gave the right to become children of God—children born not of natural descent, nor of human decision or a husband's will, but born of God."

John 1:12-13 (NIV)

An Invitation

I am inviting you to party. A really great party, and since I have some Afghan in me, I recognize a great party. It is actually a wedding. It is going to be a grand wedding, better than any wedding you have or will ever attend, including your own. I am inviting you now, but my Father God has been inviting you for quite some time now. His Son is the Bridegroom, and He is marrying His Bride when His Father says it's time, and all is ready.

Lots of people have been invited. In fact, everyone has. We all get invitations, and it is up to us whether or not we attend. We have been given the free will by God to choose how we will respond to this invitation. This invitation is never forced; you do not have to accept it. Many people will be too busy with their own lives, doing their own things, and going about their own business to even be bothered with this invitation. Some are too distracted in their daily lives to think about or plan ahead for their own future. They make plans only for today. Some will see this invitation as an insult or view it as an imposition. They will respond in anger and with ill will. Some will go a step further and harm the one that invites them or even kill those that want to spread the invitations. But this invitation is special.

The Groom is special. He has left His Father, come down to where we are and shared with us what His Father's plan is. That plan includes Him, and it includes you and me. The Groom is Jesus, and His part of the plan was to be born of a virgin mother with a Holy God as His Father. He lived a sinless life that He laid down for each and every one of us who has ever been created. Each and every one of us who is also invited to His wedding feast. He died on the cross to save us. He paid the price for our sins. He was dead and buried to rise again from the dead on the third day. He was resurrected and went back to be with His Father God. God gave us the Holy Spirit as a helper. We can talk to, and we can lean on Him. By accepting this invitation, we accept that Jesus will be our Lord and Savior. We believe in God's plan, God's Will, and God's Ways. We believe in God's Word. When we attend the wedding, we get to wear new wedding clothes so that when the

Father sees us, He sees His Son Jesus, and we get to celebrate with them. (Rather clothe yourselves in the Lord Jesus Christ. Romans 13:14)

Can you imagine what it would be like to throw a party and invite everyone, but when the party begins, there are people there that complain and fuss, make gestures of discontentment, or even wish that they were anywhere but there. The best celebrations are the ones that have everyone there that truly want to celebrate the same thing. In the case of the wedding, this wedding, it will be to celebrate the Bride and the Bridegroom. We will be a part of the Kingdom of God.

I plan to attend! How about you? What is your response to the wedding invitation? Don't know how to respond? Don't know what to wear? Don't know what to do?

He knows that. He knows everything. It is part of His plan just like you are part of His plan.

First, admit to God that you are a sinner.

It's ok, we all are sinners. We all have to admit this. The Bible says, "For all have sinned and fall short of the glory of God." Romans 3:23

Second, ask God to forgive you for your sins.

Sin leads to death. We have to repent or turn away from our old ways and turn to God and His ways. The Bible says, "For the wages of sin is death, but the gift of God is eternal life in Christ Jesus our Lord." Romans 6:23

Third, believe in Jesus and that you must be born again.

Jesus says, "I am the way and the truth and the life. No one comes to the Father except through Me." John 14:6. He also said, "I tell you the truth, unless a man is born again, he cannot see the kingdom of God." John 3:3

Fourth, believe in your heart that Jesus Christ died on the cross for you and that He rose again.

When Jesus died on the cross and rose again from the dead, He made a way for a sinful-unholy man to live forever with a sinless-Holy God. Romans 10:9-11 says it beautifully, "That if you confess with your mouth, 'Jesus is Lord,' and believe in your heart that God raised Him from the dead, you will be saved. For it is with your heart that you believe and are justified, and it is with your mouth that you confess and are saved. As the Scripture says, 'Anyone who trusts in Him will never be put to shame.'"

Fifth, you need to surrender your life to Jesus and ask Him to be both your Lord and your Savior.

This is the part where you invite Him to come into your life and into your heart. Asking Him to be your Savior means that you recognize that you are a sinner, and your sins have a price that needs to be accounted for. The cost of sin or the ultimate price to be paid for sin is death. Jesus paid the ultimate price for your sins by paying for them on the cross. He died for you. Your debt has been paid, and you stand clean, free of debt in front of God, sinless because of Jesus. He saved you from your sins. Thus He is your Savior. Asking Him to be your Lord means that you are asking Him to become Master and Teacher of your life. Where He leads you will follow. What He teaches you will learn. You are asking Him to be in a relationship with you.

If you want you can pray using your own words or pray a prayer like this:

God, I have sinned against you. I want you to forgive me for all of my sins. I believe that Jesus died on the cross for me and that He rose again. I want to surrender my life to You God. You can use me as you wish. I want Jesus to come into my life and into my heart to be my Lord and my Savior. I ask this in Jesus' name. Amen

Why do you pray in Jesus' Name? Because not only is there power in the Name of Jesus but by defining who's name you pray in means that you define to Whom you belong. For me, it is easy. I belong to Jesus, and I will joyfully pray in His Name!

Why do we say, "Amen." Because Amen means verily, verily or truly, truly. What I have just prayed I truly believe, and I verify meaning demonstrate that I believe my words to be true and accurate.

It's really very simple, but it will change your life, and you will celebrate forever.

Now is your chance to decide to attend the Wedding Feast of the Lamb of God. My prayer is this that your heart is softened, open to His calling, and His glorious plan for your future to be spent in eternity with Him! And I pray this In Jesus' Name. Amen!

Now go and put on your wedding clothes, His Name is Jesus!

"Jesus spoke to them again in parables, saying: "The kingdom of heaven is like a king who prepared a wedding banquet for his son. He sent his servant to those who had been invited to the banquet to tell them to come, but they refused to come. Then he sent some more servants and said, 'Tell those who have been invited that I have prepared my dinner: My oxen and fattened cattle have been butchered, and everything is ready. Come to the wedding banquet.' But they paid no attention and went off-one to his field, another to his business. The rest seized his servants, mistreated them and killed them. The king was enraged. He sent his army and destroyed those murderers and burned their city. Then he said to his servants, 'The wedding banquet is ready, but those I invited did not deserve to come. So go to the street corners and invite to the banquet anyone you find.' So the servants went out into the streets and gathered all the people they could find, the bad as well as the good, and the wedding hall was filled with guests. But when the king came in to see the guests, he noticed a man there who was not wearing wedding clothes. He asked, 'How did you get in here without wedding clothes, friend?' The man was speechless. Then the king told the attendants, 'Tie him hand and foot, and throw him outside, into the darkness, where there will be weeping and gnashing of teeth.' For many are invited, but few are chosen." Matthew 22:1-14 (NIV)

Books

Volume One

Born Afghan Born American Born Again

This is my testimony of leaving Islam, becoming a Christian, and living a new life in Jesus.

Volume Two

Born Muslim Became Christian Beloved Israel

This is my story of letting go of Islam, living out my Christianity, and loving my Jewish Jesus.

Volume Three

My Journey My Jesus My Joe

This is my story of being the beloved of God, falling in love with Jesus, and marrying my husband, Joe.

If you would like more information or have questions, please feel free to contact me at

www.shahesart.com

www.shahenahler.wordpress.com

My books are available at Amazon.com or ask your local bookstore to order them for you.

Printed in Great Britain
by Amazon